* 1,000,000 *
Free E-Books
@
www.ForgottenBooks.org

* Alchemy *
The Secret is Revealed
@
www.TheBookofAquarius.com

Horace Mann

And the Public School in the United States

By

Gabriel Compayre

Published by Forgotten Books 2012
Originally Published 1907

PIBN 1000377022

HORACE MANN

PIONEERS IN EDUCATION

HORACE MANN

AND THE PUBLIC SCHOOL IN THE UNITED STATES

BY

GABRIEL COMPAYRÉ

CORRESPONDENT OF THE INSTITUTE; DIRECTOR OF THE ACADEMY
OF LYONS; AUTHOR OF "PSYCHOLOGY APPLIED TO
EDUCATION," "LECTURES ON PEDAGOGY,"
"A HISTORY OF PEDAGOGY," ETC.

TRANSLATED BY

MARY D. FROST

NEW YORK
THOMAS Y. CROWELL & CO.
PUBLISHERS

Copyright, 1907,
By THOMAS Y. CROWELL & COMPANY.

Published, September, 1907.

CONTENTS AND SUMMARY

PREFACE . . . .
PREAMBLE . . . .
I. The life of Horace Mann previous to 1837. — His origin. — Poor and laborious childhood. — Precocious taste for reading. — The little library founded by Franklin. — The village school. — Mann revolts from the gloomy teachings of Calvinism. — Keen sentiment for the beauties of nature. — Family affections. — His tenderness for his mother. — His devotion to his sister. — His first marriage. — Despair caused by the loss of his wife. — His friendships. — Mann as a lawyer. — Mann as member of Congress, senator, politician. — His work for the amelioration of the treatment of the blind. — His campaign against intemperance. — Brilliancy of his public position and sadness of his private life . .
II. Horace Mann, secretary of the Board of Education of Boston (1837–1848). — Formation of the Board of Education. — Why Mann was chosen secretary of the Board. — His devotion to humanity and his love of children. — His faith in education. — Limited powers of the Board and of its secretary. — No effective authority. — No means of action except appeal to public opinion. — From the first day Mann sets to work. — Conventions. — First lecture tour. — Crusade against ignorance. — Not always an audience at his lectures. — The common school journal. — Mann acts by speech and pen. — The

twelve annual reports. — Character of these reports, genuine scholastic manifestoes. — Their historical interest. — Their pedagogic value. — Tables showing the condition of Massachusett schools in 1837. — Analyses of the twelve reports. — How Mann prepared them. — Questions addressed to competent persons. — The seventh report. — Account of European trip. — Favorable impression made upon Mann by German schools. — Somewhat excessive eulogy of German teachers. — Severe judgment on France. — Violent opposition encountered by Mann in his own country. — The non-sectarian school attacked by the American sectaries, as the French lay school was to be later. — Conflict with the Boston schoolmasters. — Reform of Boston schools. — Foundation of normal schools. — Necessity for professional training of teachers. — Pierce, master of the Lexington Normal School. — School libraries. — Importance of good books. — Other pedagogical innovations by Mann. — Lectures to teachers. — Graduated tables of the districts. — Mann's disinterestedness, his pecuniary sacrifices. — Results of his twelve years of labor. — He is elected representative from Massachusetts to the Congress at Washington. — Resigns his secretaryship 23

III. Mann's philosophy and general ideas. — No personal philosophy. — Philosophical system borrowed from George Combe. — The author of *The Constitution of Man*. — What attracted Mann in Combe's theories. — The reasons for his being a phrenologist. — The laws of the development of the mind, symmetry, and activity. — Mann's spirituality. — A strain of mysticism. — A Puritan without theology. — Faith in the immortality of the soul. — Moral psychology of Mann. — The higher faculties, conscience and the

CONTENTS AND SUMMARY

feeling of responsibility. — Intellect subordinated to feeling. — Great ideas come from the heart. — Intellectual culture subordinated to moral culture. — Utilitarian tendencies. — Universal education a social debt. — Mann's hesitation in regard to obligatory school attendance. — His eloquence. — Qualities and defects of his style. — His political views. — The honest man and good citizen. — The perils of unenlightened universal suffrage. — Without education no safety 72

IV. Horace Mann, president of Antioch College (1853-1859). — Mann elected governor of Massachusetts. — He prefers to assume the direction of Antioch College in Ohio. — His enthusiasm for this new work. — Dreams and reality. — Material difficulties. — Miserable accommodations. — Financial embarrassment. — Hostility of those about him. — His courage triumphs over all obstacles. — Organization of studies. — Selection of students. — Moral qualities preferred to intellectual gifts. — Innovations in programme and methods of instruction. — Principles of discipline. — Punishments to be avoided. — Pupils governed by appealing to their conscience. — Liberal regime. — Mann's moral authority. — What he had retained of the Puritanism of his ancestors. — His campaign against tobacco and alcoholic liquors. — Experiment in coeducation. — Failing health. — Financial ruin of the college. — Mann's final efforts. — His death 95

V. Mann's influence and the Spread of his Work. — What would distress Mann, were he to return to this world, in the present conditions. — What would rejoice him, on the other hand. — Progress of education in the United States. — It has not ceased to conform to Mann's ideas. — The Boston Board of Education led to the creation of a central organ of school administration in all the States. — That progress has advanced slowly. — Present statistics of schools in the United States. — Increase of high schools. — Influence of Mann over his contemporaries. — His greatest disciple, Henry Barnard. — That France has been inspired by the ideas and example of Mann. — Horace Mann and Felix Pecaut . . . 123

BIBLIOGRAPHY 133

PREFACE

"WITHOUT any question," Americans say, "the noblest figure in the history of education in our country is that of Horace Mann." He owes this preeminence, not only to the brilliancy of his talents and the authority of his genius, but to the circumstances, the surroundings, in which his talents and genius were called upon to play their part. He may be said to have been *"the right man in the right place,"* and we must add, also, "at the right time."

The admiration so justly awarded to Mann by his countrymen has not been denied him abroad. Felix Pecaut, to speak of no one else, has said of him: "I wish that Mann's biography might be placed in the hands, not only of all professors, but of all their pupils."

It is this biography which we offer here, in its essential features: the biography of a man admirable in many ways, for candor and purity of soul, for nobility of character, for his devotion to the cause of education and progress, for his kindness of heart no less than for the wealth of a marvellous intelligence, and, above all, for the extent of his activities and the greatness of his scholastic work.

It is especially as a man of action that Mann was incomparable. Undoubtedly, it was his good fortune to appear at the right moment, just as a widespread movement was abroad, impelling all good citizens to forward the cause of popular education. But to him belongs the credit of accelerating this movement and of leading it with the ardor and enthusiasm of an apostle — one not merely devoted to his work, but passionately absorbed in it. He was the eloquent orator of the cause of popular education, its preacher and tribune, more concerned, moreover, with the moral conduct of men than with pure science or theoretic speculation.

"Call the astronomer from the heights of heaven," he cried to his countrymen; "bring the geologist from the depths of the earth; silence all political and religious controversies; assemble all the wisdom, talent, and authority that you possess, and then begin to teach the people."

But he did not confine himself to arousing and enlightening public opinion by his ardent preaching, to conquering and inspiring it by his faith in progress and humanity; he was also a skilful organizer, a practical innovator, an indefatigable laborer for the reform of education in his country; and if he did not aspire to build up a theory, a philosophy of education, he did better still, — he created a school system. In that respect he was a great pedagogical founder. ‹ Mann died fifty years ago, but his spirit is still alive and present in the public schools of the United States. And not in America only, but in Europe, and especially in France, scholastic institutions have been inspired by his thought.\ The recent history of the establishment of French lay schools recalls in more than one respect the organization of the American common school as Mann undertook and carried it into execution a half century ago. And this resemblance, this community of views upon education between the two republics, the younger of which has followed, somewhat tardily, perhaps, but with equal ardor, in the steps of her great sister, are sufficient to revive our interest in a study of the great American educator.

Mann did not work for his own country alone, he labored for humanity, and, above all, for republican humanity. He was working for republican principles when he wrote his great address on "The Necessity for Education in a Republic," when he said, "In a republic, ignorance is a crime." He wrought for humanity, — he who, a few days before his death, addressed to his beloved pupils these last words, "Be ashamed to die before you have won some victory for humanity."

HORACE MANN

THE true life of Horace Mann, the life of an apostle of popular education, began in 1837, when he was already forty years of age. Appointed at that date secretary of the Boston Board of Education, to reorganize the school system of the State of Massachusetts, he entered upon his new functions with extraordinary ardor and intense energy. "Life," he said, "assumes a value in my eyes which I never before suspected." Up to this time he had been a gifted lawyer and a man of influence in politics, he was now to become an educator. After pleading before the bar of his country in hundreds of private causes, nearly all of which he won, he was about to take in hand the great cause of humanity at large, — of universal education. The public school became his idol; "the greatest discovery," he called it, "ever made by man." During the twelve years that he held this position, he multiplied speeches and pamphlets; he expended his strength in conventions and newspaper work. In answer to his appeals schools sprang into being where there had been none before, and those already existing set about reforming their methods; school committees revived their lukewarm zeal; a generous ardor took possession of his countrymen, kindling their blood and arousing them from their inertia. It was, in short, a renaissance, a resurrection, a revival of the American public school. It was even more than this, — it was an actual creation, a new and almost final reorganization of the system of public education, as the United States has maintained and developed it, for over half a century.

But before showing what Horace Mann accomplished, we must relate briefly how he was fitted by education and character for this great work.

The Life of Horace Mann previous to 1837

NOTHING in Mann's family and antecedents, nor in his childhood and youth, gives promise of the high destiny to which he was called, — that of a hero of education; nothing, unless it be a precocious will power and a feverish ardor for knowledge. Born on a farm in Norfolk County on the 4th of May, 1796, twenty years after the Declaration of Independence of the United States, here he lived until his twentieth year, engaged in the labors of the farm. "My childhood was not a happy one," he often said later. The death of his father in 1809, when he was only thirteen years old, impoverished this humble household still more. He was obliged to work harder than ever to support the family, — a task in which his mother set him the example. "She was," we are told, "one of those sober, sensible, energetic New England women who bring to the dull, ceaseless routine of domestic drudgery the will and courage of actual heroines."

Horace Mann educated himself by his own personal efforts amid the solitude of the country and by daily intercourse with nature. His taste for reading developed early, and a fortunate circumstance contributed to it. The little town of Franklin, one of those raw, newly built American towns which seem to have sprung from the soil like mushrooms, poor as it was in resources of every kind, possessed the embryo of a library, which it owed to the generosity of the great American for whom it was named. Franklin has somewhere related that he first thought of presenting a bell as an appropriate godfather's gift to the newborn hamlet. He changed his mind, however, on reflecting that the people of that region, as he knew them, preferred sense to sound, and he accordingly sent them a collection of books.

Mann profited by this decision; on such trifles do human affairs depend. If Franklin had been a less judicious benefactor of the town to which he stood sponsor, Mann's lot might have turned out quite differently. He might have vegetated, ignorant and obscure, in his native village and never have been able to say in later life: "If it were in my power, I would scatter books broadcast over the land, as the sower scatters grain in the furrows of the field." The supply of books presented by Franklin, chiefly works of theology and ancient history, were, it is true, soon exhausted, but not before they had kindled the sacred fire in Mann's soul. In order to purchase others, the boy spent the small sums which he could earn with his own hands by weaving straw during the long winter evenings and selling his basket work. It was his solitary reading which turned the little rustic into a well-informed youth. The township of Franklin boasted, indeed, a school, which Mann attended when he could be spared from the work of the farm; that is to say, about eight or ten weeks of the year. But what a school! Mere mechanical teaching of the three R's, a simple exercise of memory, without the slightest appeal to the intelligence; a school, in short, which awaited, like so many others, the reforms which Mann was to introduce at a later day.

The village church, in the quality of its religious instruction, was worth even less than the school. It was conducted by a fanatical preacher, Dr. Evans, an extra- or hyper-Calvinist, as Mann called him, whose only aim was to terrorize his flock by dismal pictures of future punishment in the next world. The youthful Mann, with the docility of his childish imagination, trembled and shuddered like the rest under these terrifying threats of eternal perdition. But an event was to occur, which completely revolutionized his ideas. At the age of twelve he lost a brother whom he tenderly loved, and in the anguish of his grief the boy learned to reflect. Guided by his heart, sustained by his growing reason, he was seized by an instinct of rebellion; he said to himself that it was not possible that his beloved brother should have to endure eternal punishment in another world; that the God he worshipped was not a monster of cruelty. He had reached a moment of moral crisis, almost such a night as Jauffray describes. "I remember, as if it were yesterday," he said long after, "the day, the hour, the place, the circumstances, in which I broke the chains which had bound me." From that hour dated for Mann the awakening of mind which was to lead to a sincere but very broad religious faith, moral rather than theological, and free from servitude to dogmas, of which some one has said: "What would be called religion in others, was morality in Mann."

Mann's early education had been acquired a little at random, like that of Rousseau, but in the absolutely pure and innocent atmosphere of country life. It was from a wandering professor that he learned the rudiments of Latin. An ardent reader, he was at the same time a fervent worshipper of nature; he loved to watch a glorious sunrise, and at night stretched out on a grassy meadow to "feast his eyes on the starry heavens."

He had an intense natural love of beauty, and later, when he had become a pedagogue, he did not conceal his distrust of a purely bookish education. "It is a great mistake," he said, "to be a slave to books. The secret of education is not love of books, but love of knowledge."

A poet lay dormant in him — he himself has said so — a tender enthusiastic poet who reveals himself in his flights of oratory and in his literary style, whether by dazzling wealth of imagery or by the lyrical expression of noble sentiments. Proud and high-souled, he was at the same time the most sensitive of men, uniting rare energy with deep tenderness of nature. When in his later life he was called upon at times to reprimand an unruly pupil, it was with difficulty that he could restrain his tears.

In his family relations he showed the most exquisite delicacy of feeling; while his frankness and tenderness of nature gave infinite charm to his friendship.

For thirty years he lived with his mother, taking care to shield her from all knowledge of his griefs and perplexities lest they should sadden her, and seeking by every means in his power to make her life tranquil and happy. "The most exquisite emotion I have ever felt," he writes, "was in observing my mother's face brighten and her step grow lighter on hearing something good said of me, and to feel that this change in her bearing proceeded from a secret well-spring of pleasure which I had touched in her heart."

One of the joys of his life was to return to Franklin and revisit the scenes of his childhood. He often made pilgrimages thither, and saw with emotions of melancholy the paternal roof, which had passed into strangers' hands.

"Here lived my father whom I dimly remember and my mother whose memory is so much a part of me, and of whom I can say that if there is any good in me, I owe it to her."

Two noble filial souls have expressed the same sentiments in kindred language at an interval of fifteen centuries. "From my father," said Marcus Aurelius, "I inherit modesty; to my mother I owe my piety."

Mann carried into his friendships the same tenderness as into his family ties. The list is long of the distinguished men with whom he held fraternal relations. Let us name first Dr. Howe, who has been called the Lafayette of Greek independence, having served as surgeon-in-chief to the Greek army and navy during the revolution of 1822, and who, on his return to America, devoted himself to founding and developing institutions for the blind, the deaf and dumb, and the feeble-minded. (It was he who educated the famous deaf, dumb, and blind girl, Laura Bridgman.)

Channing, the celebrated leader of the Unitarian body, to which Mann himself belonged,[1] was also among his friends, as was Theodore Parker, the only preacher whom he enjoyed hearing, and who once wrote to him: "Spare your strength; remember that if you kill yourself, it will take the Lord a long time to give us another Horace Mann."

To this list belongs also George Combe, the philosopher, of whom Mann was the disciple as well as friend, and many more to whom he was bound by community of sentiments and an equal enthusiasm for the cause of popular education. Edward Everett, who had been appointed governor of Massachusetts, actively seconded his efforts, as did Senator Sumner and the mayor of Boston, Josiah Quincy.

---

[1] The sect of Unitarians, whose origin we must seek in the England of the seventeenth century, is the most liberal of American religious bodies. Its followers admit revelation without accepting all its dogmas. There are no less than 600 Unitarian congregations in America at the present day.

For his sister Mann cherished the warmest affection and a devotion of which he gave proof by coming to her aid in a serious crisis and saving her husband, a merchant who had failed in business, from financial ruin. She remained all her life the intimate confidante of his thoughts.

What shall be said of his worship of her whom he had chosen as the companion of his life, and who was suddenly snatched from him by death after two brief years of perfect happiness? He had married her in 1831 after an engagement of ten years. Her loss left in his heart a wound that was long in healing. In his first grief he wrote: "My whole life was centred in the home which she brightened by her presence.[1] She imparted to me renewed strength for my work and inspired me with fresh motives for courageous activity. I should never end if I attempted to describe the revelation of moral beauty that flowed from her life and the grace of feeling which sprang like a delicate flower from the adamant of her virtues."

The public-spirited citizen was in no respect inferior to the son, brother, and husband. As a lawyer Mann made it a rule to accept only just causes and to plead only for the truth; as a mem-

[1] Mann's first wife was the daughter of Dr. Messer of Brown University, where he had been a student.

ber of the legislature and senator he rose above party politics, speaking only in behalf of public interests and great philanthropic causes.

In 1816, at the age of twenty, Mann had become a regular student at Brown University, a small college founded in 1764 in the city of Providence. In order to pay his matriculation fees, he gave lessons as a tutor during the vacations, thus following a custom still prevalent among the poor students of American colleges, some of whom are reduced to the necessity of paying their way by seeking service as hotel waiters and the like during the summer. At Brown, Mann studied law, and distinguished himself at once among his companions. His masters bore witness that he was the best student in the university and, at the same time, the best whist player.

One trait already characterizes Mann's turn of mind and natural trend of thought,—he chose for his last scholastic thesis the following subject: "On the Progressive Character of the Human Race." It is this belief in progress, in the indefinite development of the moral and intellectual faculties of man, which was to be the watchword of his whole life and the motive of all his actions.[1]

---

[1] Another of Mann's youthful writings was entitled "On the Duty of every American toward Posterity."

On the conclusion of his studies and after having held for some time a professorship of Latin and Greek literature at Brown University, Mann settled in Dedham, a small Massachusetts town, where he entered upon the practice of the law, pleading cases before the Norfolk and Boston bars. He was already in full possession of his oratorical powers. He was, according to the testimony of his biographers, a redoubtable orator, with a terrible power of sledge-hammer retorts, which he hurled at his adversaries like bombshells thrown into an enemy's camp. On the occasion of the national holiday, the 4th of July, 1824, Mann delivered an address which attracted the notice of John Quincy Adams,[1] future President of the United States, the same whom Mann was to succeed twenty-five years later as member of the House of Representatives.

His reputation grew from year to year, until he had become the most highly esteemed lawyer in that region. It was in 1827 that the confidence of the electors of Norfolk County called him to a seat in the State legislature of Massachusetts.

---

[1] John Quincy Adams was President of the United States from 1825-1829. A few years after the expiration of his term as President, he was elected member of Congress from Massachusetts and continued to be elected until he died.

In 1830 he was elected State senator, then president of the Senate in 1836.

The part he took in political assemblies was always a brilliant one. He preached as often as possible what he called his "gospel of temperance and education." But his idealism did not divert him from a due concern for the material interests of his country. His two first speeches in Congress were respectively upon religious liberty and upon railroads. But the subjects which chiefly occupied his energies at this period, when he was in the habit of working sixteen hours a day, were the establishment of a lunatic asylum and the campaign against intemperance. After five years of constant effort Mann obtained from the House a vote for necessary funds to erect a commodious and suitable building, the Worcester asylum, where two hundred and thirty insane patients were to be received, treated with gentleness and humanity, and employed in agricultural pursuits. "We have overthrown the dungeons of inhumanity," he exclaimed, on accomplishing this work; "the outworks are stormed at least, and some of the unhappy prisoners can now enjoy the beauty of the physical world, and before long I hope they will share the benefits of the moral world." In this humanitarian enterprise Mann was not merely a promoter, but, charged with organizing it personally, he gave proof of those administrative talents which he was to display some years later in his scholastic campaign. Let us add that he found excellent associates to aid him; among others a woman, "the adorable" Miss Dix, to whom he paid this signal homage:

"If Queen Victoria in one of her triumphal progresses through her states were to encounter this more than sovereign American woman on one of her charitable progresses, it is the former, not the latter, who ought to bend the knee and kiss the other's hand. Yes, the empress of so many millions of mankind should bow before this angel from heaven, sent down for the salvation of poor insane men and women."

Mann was no less fortunate in his struggle against intemperance. Himself one of the most temperate of men, I do not know whether he had sworn to his mother, like Lincoln, never to touch intoxicating liquors, but he did, in fact, abstain from doing so, lamenting that he found so few imitators. To plant a school near every dwelling and to remove the saloon, such was his plan. "How many thousands of drunkards would never have become so if the saloon had been five miles away from their home!"

In 1832 Mann proposed a law forbidding the public sale of intoxicating liquors, at least on Sundays. The project received but two favorable votes, including, no doubt, his own. But he was not the man to let himself be discouraged by a first failure; and thanks to his tenacity and his eloquence, the law was passed in 1837 by two hundred and forty votes to seventeen in the House of Representatives and twenty-three to six in the Senate. Thus fortune smiled on Mann's political career; he had become a power in the Massachusetts legislature, but beneath this brilliant surface, his private life held much of sadness. Since 1833 his home had been desolate, and he had never become reconciled to his loss. In the private journal to which he was accustomed to confide every evening the events of his life and his inmost thoughts, he speaks sadly of "days devoid of consolation and sleepless, tearful nights." Poverty had pursued him even amid his successes at the bar and in the House. Who could have imagined that for a period of six months the brilliant statesman, the busy lawyer, had only the means of dining once in two days. At this time he denied himself and incurred heavy debts in order to help his brother-in-law, who had failed. His health, which had been undermined by labor and privations, grew daily worse, so that his friends at one time despaired of his life; and this man of forty-one years, who appeared to be broken down and utterly crushed, was about to recover his strength and energies at the call of an inner voice which summoned him to act in behalf of humanity, — in behalf of education for the people. He was about to devote himself exclusively to the cause of education and to enter upon a campaign in favor of schools, — a campaign of twelve years full of sacrifices and efforts, the noblest, assuredly, which the annals of education have to offer us.

II

HORACE MANN, SECRETARY OF THE BOSTON BUREAU OF EDUCATION

ON the 20th of April, 1837, Mann, in his capacity of president of the Massachusetts Senate, signed an official act relating to public schools which was to decide the future course of his life. By this act a board of education was established, whose primal object was to study and investigate the moral and material condition of the schools in order, subsequently, to discover and apply the best methods of improving them, the board being thus both an examining and a reforming body. A few months later Mann was appointed its secretary, and this modest title was to enable him to become for a long period the capable and indefatigable agent for the reorganization of the school system of his country.[1]

It was a great change in his life; he now became the advocate for all men. "Let my new clients,

[1] Channing, the leading Unitarian divine, wrote to him: "I hear that you are about to devote yourself to the cause of education in our Republic. I rejoice over it."

the rising generation, come to me," he said. From the outset he had traced for himself a line of moral conduct,—"May God grant me to subdue my egotism and give me wisdom of mind and kindness of heart,"—and at the same time he set before himself a course of action which he was to carry out as faithfully as the former. He sketched it in these terms in a letter to his sister: "If I can be the instrument of a reform which will settle how schools can be better taught, what are the best books, the best plans of study, the best methods of education; if I can discover by what means a child who does not speak, who does not think, who does not reflect, can surely become by means of education a noble citizen, ready to fight for the right and die for it, may I not flatter myself with the hope that I have not labored in vain?"

And with that power of imagination which made the most distant events present to him, which showed him the future as if it already existed, he dreamed of the harvest while he was sowing the seed. He beheld his beloved Massachusetts covered with flourishing schools, the other States of the Union following her example, and the whole human race regenerated by education!

The faith which animated him was early implanted in his soul; it was drawn from a double source, — his devotion to men and his love of children. No one has spoken of childhood more tenderly than he:

"How engaging children are in their happy unconsciousness! Ignorant, when they must have knowledge in order to live; absorbed in the present, when they are embarked for eternity; blind in the midst of perils; as unconscious of the noble enthusiasms and ardent passions which slumber in their breasts as the cloud is of the storm and thunder it hides in its bosom, — such are these cherished beings whose future is in our hands. . . ."

Let us quote one more charming passage:

"How did this fair child come to us so full of music and poetry? Who put a whole dancing-school into his steps? At the least sound which arouses his gayety, he seems to throw off the law of gravitation; he floats, he glides as if his body were a light feather and his soul a breeze playing with it. The child is the greatest of miracles! . . ."

How many times before becoming secretary of the Board of Education had Mann addressed to his countrymen moving appeals in behalf of instruction, such as he was about to renew unceasingly until he had brought them to feel as he did, until he had made them realize the importance of education, until he had carried them with him, so that all should resolve to shed light and truth upon mankind "as God sheds sunshine and rain upon the earth!"

"How is this?" he cried. "If some one should bring you word to-morrow that he had found a coal mine which would bring in ten per cent, would you not hasten to invest in it? And yet here are men who might bring you in forty or fifty per cent, and you leave them grovelling in ignorance. You know how to make use of plants and animals, you can produce wheat from herd's-grass and turn the jackal into a dog; . . . and you have children of whom you can make nothing!

"You build hospitals, you establish law-courts. Why? To punish people for the ignorance which has made them criminals; to harbor poor wretches who have failed here below for lack of instruction. But are you not yourselves the unconscious authors and accomplices of these evils which you vainly seek to prevent or to cure? Build schools then; you will thus abolish ignorance, crime, and misery. You will quench hatred and make the happiness and greatness of the nation through the prosperity and morality of each of its citizens."

The aim which Mann was pursuing by his personal efforts he had long since proposed to his countrymen. He had dreamed of it during his thoughtful childhood on the shores of the ocean, during his youth at Brown University when he delivered essays on human progress, in his manhood when he sat in the legislature. But at the moment when he was himself intrusted with the accomplishment of his dream, anxiety mingled with his enthusiasm. Men of ability are apt to distrust their own talents and powers. Should he prove capable of carrying on so great a mission and succeeding in an enterprise which was partly technical? "I tremble," he writes in his diary, "at the idea of this task which has fallen to me." His adversaries reproached him, in fact, with a lack of scholastic experience. He had been, it is true, a tutor in Providence and a member of the school committee in Dedham. But these were slender qualifications beside the professional claims of his competitor for the office, Professor Carter, a teacher of long experience. The governing powers of Massachusetts must have been fully persuaded of the preeminence of Mann's moral qualities when they chose him in preference to such a candidate. They had divined what miracles were to be expected from his untiring devotion and from such rare nobility of soul united with such admirable energy. Mann amply justified their confidence, and afforded one more proof that it is not always one of the trade, a professional, but on the contrary, an outsider who most frequently accomplishes the great reforms in education.

That which added to the difficulties of Mann's work was the nature of the duties intrusted to him. Neither he nor the Board was invested with any executive power. He did not have that actual authority over schools and instructors which the State of New York, for instance, conferred on its superintendent of schools, an office created in 1835.

The Boston Board deliberated, gave advice, expressed its wishes, but did not direct in school affairs. But the worth of institutions depends upon the men who form part of them. With a leader like Mann, who was its soul, the Board of Education exercised a decisive action, an extraordinary influence, over the school districts of Massachusetts and later of the whole Union, such as ministers of public instruction in other countries might have reason to envy. The following detail clearly shows how conscientiously Mann proceeded to fulfil the duties of his position. Before setting to work he entered upon a sort of pedagogical retreat, devoting a certain time to retirement and meditation. For several weeks he shut himself up in company with books on education; he read and pondered over Miss Edgeworth's *Practical Education* and *The Necessity for Popular Education* by Dr. James Simpson. He took great pleasure in this reading, which he pronounced "delightful," and which furnished him with a store of new ideas. He convinced himself more and more fully that the educational mission on which he had entered was the one that best suited his tastes, feelings, and principles. This period of retirement and reflection was not of long duration, however. Mann received his appointment as secretary on the 30th of June, 1837. By the 28th of August of the same year he had opened the campaign with his first lecture tours. It was a brilliant beginning. In each of the fourteen counties of Massachusetts, Mann assembled conventions of all the friends of education, teachers, members of school committees from the three hundred districts in the State, leading members of the community; in short, all who were eager to listen to the burning words of the great educator. Mann well knew that his first mission was to win souls, to arouse good-will, to create a current of opinion, to communicate to others the enthusiasm with which he was himself possessed. It was at this price only that he could hope for success. He must obtain the moral support of all those interested in the reform of schools, rouse from their torpor the old school committees, whose origin dated back to the seventeenth century. He must also secure the material support of wealthy citizens, from whom he solicited donations while awaiting the moment when these private liberalities should arouse the emulation of the State, from which he hoped later to obtain funds to endow the various scholastic establishments which he proposed to found.

On the one hand, he must influence public opinion to desire and demand the necessary reforms; on the other hand, he must induce the legislatures of the country to vote for them and carry them into execution. A minister of education would have been able to draw up orders and sign decrees; Mann could only call conventions and draw up reports. His position can be defined by saying that he was before all, not a philosopher, not a practical instructor, but a soldier, a tribune of education, a missionary who journeyed from town to town, from village to village, spreading his ideas and his faith, a Peter the Hermit preaching a crusade against ignorance. On his lecture tours Mann lavished his eloquence like an American Jean Mace, — a Jean Mace of greater powers as an orator and loftier flights. He often addressed different audiences for twenty-five successive days.

In that free American democracy which contains so many kings,—railroad kings, petroleum kings, and the rest,—Mann was the lecture king. We have since seen presidential candidates in the United States multiply themselves to a still greater extent, and under the spur of ambition pour forth an even greater number of speeches, but in the matter of scholastic addresses, disinterested speeches in the cause of education, Mann undoubtedly holds the record, not for his own country alone, but for the whole world.

We must not imagine, however, that he met with constant success in these oratorical campaigns, which he carried on with so fine an ardor. His annual lecture trip was not invariably a triumphal progress. On one occasion he had an audience consisting of three ladies; another day, a humiliating day, he found himself alone! He owns sadly that political speeches would have been better attended. "Politics," he added, "are the only god of this people." And he adds jestingly, "If a mob collects anywhere, instead of reading the riot act to disperse it, one has only to announce a lecture on education; that will be sufficient — not a soul will remain."

Let us add that Mann, although a born orator, never addressed an audience without fear and trembling. He had, moreover, to contend against physical weakness. On the eve of delivering three or four lectures in succession, he writes in his diary, "Alas for my poor body!"

He carried on this propaganda with his pen as well as by speeches; he began publishing in 1838 a scholastic newspaper called the *Common School Journal,* which he continued to conduct for ten years. He there set forth in detail his views on special questions relating to teaching and educational methods. He thus led the way for all the pedagogical journals which have since flourished in the United States; notably, the *Journal of Education* which Barnard, the Horace Mann of Connecticut, edited for thirty-one years. But it was, above all, by the publication of his reports that Mann exercised a marked influence on public opinion. The twelve statements which he drew up year after year are a genuine pedagogical monument. They occupied about a thousand pages in the edition of his works. Issued in a large edition, about twenty thousand copies, they were circulated in all directions, read in remote hamlets as well as in great cities; people learned from them what schools were and what they ought to be. Officially addressed to the Board of Education, they were in reality destined for the people, whom it was urgent to instruct as to the importance of education. In short, they were veritable scholastic manifestoes summoning public opinion to provide instruction for the people.

Thus Mann's annual reports resume twelve years of intense labor and fruitful results; they have, in the first place, historic interest, exhibiting as they do the scholastic situation of the period before proceeding to relate what Mann did or attempted to do to improve it. If in the final pages of these reports he can justly celebrate the progress brought about by twelve years of labor, he frankly admits at the outset the condition of weakness and poverty into which the three hundred schools of Massachusetts had fallen.[1] The fault lay especially with the school committees, which fulfilled but negligently the wide functions which existing legislation had intrusted to them. They were to choose text-books, to decide upon the children too poor to purchase them, — to

[1] The history of American education proves how powerless the laws are when they are in advance of the manners and habits of a people. When Mann set about his work it was more than two hundred years since the first colonists of America had resolved to establish a sytem of gratuitous instruction (1630) and of obligatory instruction (1642). In 1647 it had already been decided that there should be a primary school for every fifty families, and a higher school for every hundred families, but nothing of the kind existed.

whom they should be furnished gratuitously, — to visit each school once a month. It was also their mission to preside over the choice of teachers, and to make sure that those selected were the best it was possible to secure "as guardians of that inestimable treasure, — the children of the district." But ineffectual as are our own school committees (appointed to insure the execution of the law of obligatory attendance) the American committees seem to have discharged their duties very little better. School inspections were not carried out seriously. The committee man too often contented himself with a brief call in the course of a country drive or a business trip, during which he fastened his horse at the gate, entered the schoolhouse to rest and warm himself, and this done, his inspection was over.

Like a physician who thoroughly studies all the symptoms of a disease before attempting its cure, Mann took careful note of all the defects and vices of the system he was attempting to reform, and in the highly unflattering picture he draws of the situation, he addresses many reproaches to the committees. They do not pay sufficient attention, he says, to the choice of schoolbooks, and they authorize too great a number; they do not take sufficient precautions in nominating teachers, of whom two-thirds are incapable, not having passed the examinations required by law. The school attendance is most irregular, a third of the pupils being absent during the winter months, and two-fifths during the summer; the schoolhouses are poor and out of repair; the mechanical system of instruction is the only one in favor; and, finally, the salaries of both men and women teachers are insufficient, being about twenty-five dollars for men and eleven for women. But what vexed Mann's enthusiastic soul more than all was the apathy of the people, who seemed generally indifferent to school matters and unconcerned for the education of their children; and recalling the doctrine of Cousin, "As are teachers, so are schools," the American educator proposed to alter it to, "As are parents, so are schools and teachers."

These twelve reports of Mann's are a world in themselves. All the essential questions of education are considered and settled in turn in this vast compendium of theoretical pedagogy, over which we shall cast a rapid glance. The reader will be especially struck by the breadth and largeness of Mann's views, but he will soon be made aware that the secretary of the Boston Board did not lose himself amid vague speculations. Mann was not a mere preacher of the ideal, he was an American, and consequently positive and practical; the most minute questions of material organization interest him equally with the loftiest problems of moral training; he discusses the schoolroom desks and benches with as much care and competence as the philosophic principles of discipline. In his first report, Mann deals with ventilation, lighting, and heating; he wants no more schoolrooms where the wind and rain can enter and the ink freeze in the ink-stands. He is anxious to place these, whom he calls his eighty thousand Massachusetts children, in healthful and hygienic surroundings. In his second report, he examines the methods of instruction in reading, and condemns the alphabetical process, which consists in spelling by letters, for which he would substitute the "word method," which consists in teaching combinations of syllables and words which recall to the child familiar objects and attractive ideas.

In the third report, after referring to child labor in factories, Mann points out the importance of libraries and the influence which reading exerts over the character. In the fourth, he treats of school attendance, and insists upon the necessity of dividing the pupils of each school into graded classes.

The fifth introduces us to more general questions.

Mann therein sets forth the benefits of education and shows how it enriches men materially, being not only a source of moral wealth, but "an important factor in economics." "Wealth always follows intelligence; the hand is another and a better hand when knowledge guides it." The sixth report is devoted almost exclusively to a special subject, to which Mann attached the highest importance, one of his favorite theses, — the necessity of giving physiology a place among school studies. On this point Herbert Spencer has merely followed in Mann's steps. "Whence comes it," says Mann, "that one-quarter of the children who come into the world die before reaching the age of one year, unless it results from general ignorance of the laws of life?" And still associating economic reasons with sentiments of humanity, he adds: "Infractions of physiological laws kill millions of men and destroy millions of dollars."

The seventh report, which attracted great attention, is an account of the tour which Mann made in 1843 through various European countries; he also considers here the question of corporal punishment and the difficulties arising from the excessive cultivation of the verbal memory.

In the report of 1844 Mann devotes himself to the development of an idea which was dear to him, — the employment of women as teachers; he also attacks the question of normal schools and that of the study of vocal music.

The ninth report, that of 1845, is one of the most important. Mann here points out to what motives, — school motives, — to what principles of action, discipline and moral training should in his opinion appeal. He desires that the obedience of pupils should in future be founded on affection and respect, not upon fear. He lays bare the dangers of jealousy and envy arising from emulation; and, passing from modes of discipline to methods of instruction, he follows Pestalozzi in asking that induction be substituted for deduction, the personal research of an awakened intelligence for the mechanical tasks of slavish memorizing.

In 1846, satisfied with the results so far attained, Mann allows himself to review the past and proceeds to write a history of the Massachusetts schools from their origin in those early days when the Pilgrim Fathers brought with them from Europe to the virgin soil of America their Puritan faith and their ideal of civic independence.

Returning the following year to the influence and effects of education, he shows how it can cure social evils, vices, and crimes; and, finally, in a twelfth report, the summing up and, as it were, the climax of all the rest, he raises a pæan of victory and celebrates once more the virtues of the public schools.

Assuredly the twelve reports of Mann are rather the work of a man of action, of an educational leader, than of a philosopher or a pedagogue who originates methods. But they were admirably adapted to his aim, which was to arouse the popular mind and make educational questions the order of the day in his country. "How many dead minds there are to resuscitate!" he exclaimed. Doubtless he experienced many disappointments; his flaming words often fell upon stony hearts; he was confronted with inertia and indifference. "When I am about to present my gospel of education in some new place, I feel as if I were standing in bad weather before the door of a house and vainly pulling the bell, with no one at home or all too busy to see me." But little by little, thanks to his persistence, the people awoke; the door was opened.

"There is not one city," he said, some years later, "in which I have not found warm friends of education — everywhere there are a few, in some places their name is legion." In drawing up his reports Mann first made use of his own observations, of all the facts and ideas he had collected in the course of his official tours and his personal investigations. But indefatigable worker as he was, he excelled also in the art of making others work. He caused to be sent to him each year by the school committees more than three hundred local reports,— as many as there were districts in the State; and thanks to these regular communications, he was thoroughly well posted.

But in order to inform himself still more fully, he appealed to volunteer co-workers, and applied successfully the method which has since become extremely popular in America, and which in our own day an attempt has been made to introduce into France: that of sending circulars or sets of questions upon various subjects addressed to competent persons. Thus, in 1841, he made an inquiry by correspondence into the subject of which he had treated in his fifth report. He inquired of business men, merchants, manufacturers, their opinions as to education from an economic point of view.

Similarly, in 1847, he proposed the following questions: "What influence may the school have on the morality of the pupils? Under the influence of the best systems of education which we are able to establish to-day, in what proportion can we hope that the children attending the schools will become honorable men, honest merchants, conscientious jurymen, incorruptible legislators, electors, and magistrates, good parents, good neighbors, and useful citizens? What number, on the other hand, will remain refractory to all efforts made to preserve them from vice? What proportion out of a hundred of these children are liable to become drunkards, gamblers, tramps, rioters, thieves, slanderers, murderers?" Mann distributed this circular among such of his countrymen as were best qualified to pronounce an opinion, notably to David Page, Solomon Adams, Roger Howard, Catherine Beecher. All replied that the influence of the school might be supreme, and this unanimous testimony filled Mann with delight.

Of all Mann's reports the one which attracted the most notice was the seventh, in which he gave an account of his journey to Europe in 1843. Mann had married, on the 1st of May of that year, Mary Peabody, who, like her sister Elizabeth, had devoted herself to the work of education. This European trip was their wedding journey. It was to be also a rest tour for Mann, who was so much exhausted by his labors and struggles that he had begun to ask himself whether he should have strength to carry on his work. His brain was so excited by a perpetual, feverish activity that "it worked of itself," according to an expression of Dr. Howe.

Finally, it was a tour for study, the traditional European tour, which Barnard, who constantly emulated Mann, was to accomplish in his turn two years later, in 1845. How many have since followed in their steps! During his six months of travel, Mann interested himself with a lively curiosity in all the sights which the Old World offered to his astonished eyes. His journal is full of brilliant descriptions, whether of the monuments, museums, churches, which he visited, or of the historic sights and scenery which he gazed at in passing. But it is especially the philanthropic establishments — the hospitals, prisons, houses of reform for young culprits, asylums for the blind and deaf and dumb, and, above all, the schools—which attracted his attention. On this last point he does full justice to the Old World, praising the schools of Scotland and especially those of Germany to such an extent that he seriously offended the national pride of his countrymen. At Halle he admires Francke's Institute, with its three thousand pupils, at that time under the direction of Niemeyer; and he respectfully salutes the statue of its founder, the pedestal of which bears the simple inscription: "He had faith in God."

At Darmstadt he is surprised to learn from the director of schools that fortunate Germany had no difficulties to encounter in regard to school attendance and regularity on the part of the pupils, because "German children are born with the innate idea that they are to go to school." "With us," Mann adds sadly, "the school records of present and absent prove that this instinct is unknown to the American child." In Berlin, at Groningen[1] in Prussia, in Saxony especially, Mann found occasion for praising and extolling, not perhaps without a strain of exaggeration, the qualities of German instructors.

"All the defects of the German schools," he wrote, "find their corrective in the qualities of the masters. If one could bring together all those whom I have visited in their schools, they would form one of the finest assemblages of men I have ever met. Full of intelligence, of dignity, and gentleness, they give by their manners and bearing the impression of conscientious devotion to duty. In our American schools, where we often

[1] In these two cities, Mann, who had always been deeply interested in the deaf and dumb language, ascertained that articulate speech had already been substituted for the old system of a sign language. On his return to America, he attempted to popularize the use of the new method, but without success. Articulate speech was not to be introduced in America until twenty-six years later, when it was taught in Boston.

have recourse to women as teachers, one of the chief arguments in favor of this practice is that women are gentler, more affectionate and encouraging than men. In Germany this argument would not be understood, or rather the facts which justify it with us do not exist there. Indeed, I have never seen in the German schools a single instance of harshness or severity; all is encouragement, animation, sympathy. I have seen hundreds of schools and thousands of pupils, but I have never met one pupil who underwent punishment in my presence."

There is certainly some exaggeration here; gentleness has never been claimed as the chief quality of German schoolmasters. In the presence of the visiting inspector or of a stranger taking notes, teachers and pupils are alike on their guard and do not always show themselves in their true light. With some naivete Mann judged by appearances. He was also delighted to observe what joy the German masters manifested when their pupils replied correctly to the questions put to them. "I have seen a master in his gratification at a correct answer clasp his pupil in his arms and caress him with paternal tenderness, as if unable to repress his joyful emotion. . . ."

Mann fortunately discovered other more interesting and genuine features of German education: the methods by which reading was taught, writing treated as a branch of drawing, geography associated with history and the natural sciences, the importance accorded to singing in schools.

Enthusiastic over Germany to such an extent that some of his countrymen, on reading his account of his journey, nicknamed him "the Prussian," Mann was, on the other hand, decidedly severe toward the French schools. We need not wonder at this; for in spite of the progress achieved since the Guizot law was passed in 1833, we were still at that time far behind Germany. The French character seems, moreover, to have inspired in him more distrust than sympathy. Ten years later, in 1853, after the Napoleonic *coup d'etat*, he wrote to his friend Combe: "What do you think of France? Frivolity, sensualism, Catholicism — from these three causes united, what may not be the issue debasing to humanity?"

In 1843 Mann could see in our people only their defects: the military spirit of a nation eager for glory and conquest, heir to the ambitions of a Napoleon — and yet he visited France during the peaceful reign of Louis Philippe. Read, for example, what he writes after a visit to the park and palace of Versailles, of which he remarks, however, that they surpass in extent and splendor all that he has yet seen in Europe. "The palace of Versailles contains a gallery where the history of France is told in painting. One sees there pictures representing all Napoleon's great battles, portraits of marshals of France, admirals, and kings. Everything breathes of war; a warlike flame blows over it; all is red with the blood of battles. You would call it rather a temple dedicated to Mars than the work of a civilized nation in the nineteenth century of the so-called Christian era. We should have said beforehand that it was impossible for such a work to have been conceived, but when we know the French character thoroughly, we say, on the contrary, that it was impossible for such a work not to have been done. It is only at rare intervals that we come across some scattered memorials which recall the philosophers, the sages, the philanthropists. All this is done merely to cultivate and develop a passion for the criminal glory of war. . . ."

If Mann were living now, he would perhaps be obliged to modify somewhat his judgment of France and it is for American imperialism that he would doubtless reserve some of his bitterest censures. On the whole, he returned from his travels with mingled impressions. The moral situation of Europe, its political and social institutions, were not of a nature to suit either his republicanism or his virtue. He saw in them the result of long centuries of ignorance, superstition, and tyranny; he was aghast at the immorality displayed in the great cities.

"The children in certain quarters of Manchester and London are surrounded by such baleful influences and such abominable examples that they may be said to have been born to be imprisoned, transported, or hung as surely as wheat grows to be eaten."

And so from the heart of Europe, seeing all its vices at close range and recalling America only by its virtues, he reverted with pride to the memories of his beloved country; he evoked the shades of the forefathers landing on Plymouth Rock; he venerated them as if they had carried away from Europe all the goodness there when they set forth to build schoolhouses and churches amid the newly cleared forests, that they might thus keep the sacred flames of learning and piety still burning.

On his return to Boston, however, Mann was destined to discover once again that all was not for the best in the best of Americas, that the noblest intentions could be misunderstood and travestied there, and that the spirit of piety inherited from the Puritan forefathers might also have its defects and inconveniences. In the genuine ardor of his convictions, he had perhaps dreamed of a progress without opposition, a mild and peaceable administration inspired by his kindly spirit and eagerly accepted by all. He was soon undeceived; violent opposition and bitter quarrels awaited him, partly religious and political, and partly professional. It was especially after his European trip that the storm burst; but from the start Mann's work had been confronted by bitter opponents, among whom was the Rev. Mr. Smith, a rabid Calvinist, who reminded him by his fanaticism of Parson Evans of the Franklin church, and whom he dubbed "an indomitable hyena."

History, it is said, repeats itself from age to age. What is not less true is, that it repeats itself from country to country. Separated by oceans though they may be, the same plants spring up, the same passions rage on either shore. Mann encountered in his country the same violent opposition which in our own day and our own land have prevailed against the organizers of common school or primary instruction. In the Massachusetts of fifty years ago, as in France for the last twenty years, sectarians have declaimed against what they call "godless schools." The organization of the public school, of the American "civic school," as Mann conceived it, strongly resembles in its origin the establishment of lay schools in France. Up to the beginning of the nineteenth century, the schools of New England, the old Puritan schools, had remained subject to the Church; the ministers of religion visited them frequently and gave instruction in the catechism. Calvinism, at that time the dominant, in fact, the only faith, reigned supreme. The *New England Primer*, the reading-book placed in the hands of the children, was steeped in Calvinist doctrines.

For this sectarian school ruled by the Church, or rather the churches, since orthodoxy had become dismembered into several distinct sects,—Mann had sought to substitute an undenominational school, religious still, no doubt, since he recommended the reading of the Bible and esteemed it a work of inestimable value in forming the characters of the young,—but independent of all denominational teaching and severed from those sects which divided between them the dominion over souls.

In France, it is the philosophical and lay mind which has succeeded tardily in separating the school and the Church; in the United States, it is from the diversity of religious beliefs, from the multiplicity of Christian churches, that the same movement has emanated. As long as Calvinism was dominant, there had been no difficulty in accepting the teaching of one exclusive doctrine in the schools; but when Baptists, Methodists, Episcopalians, Congregationalists, and Unitarians began to divide the allegiance of the Christian congregations, each of these sects, being no longer able to rule alone in the schools, naturally sought to eliminate all rival beliefs and to secularize instruction in the public schools, open as they were to children of all sects and conditions.

But this logical conclusion, to which the diversity of religious opinions would seem to lead, was not yet admitted in Mann's time. The orthodox sects, moreover, had not yet resigned themselves to the loss of their supremacy. Mann was an object of suspicion in their eyes,—he was a Unitarian; that is to say, what the most advanced liberal Protestants are with us. He eliminated creeds and was at bottom a rationalist, remaining a Christian in spirit only, not according to the letter.

Did he not give the worst possible example to the young by abstaining from attendance at public worship? It was remarked that on a certain

Sunday he had failed to be present at any religious service in the city where he had gone to lecture: this was regarded as intolerable. Mann excused himself, and perhaps aggravated his offence, by remarking that as there were three churches of different faiths in the town in question and he had not attended any of them, he had committed the offence with which he was charged three times over.

As to the essential basis of the discussion, he reminded his opponents that the legislative act of 1827 had interdicted in the American schools the use of books imbued with the spirit of any sect whatever, and that accordingly he was, on the whole, conforming to the law. Already in 1840 the sectarians in Massachusetts had opened the conflict against Mann in the legislature. His friend Everett was no longer there to defend him. The moment appeared a favorable one for attacking the liberals, as a wind of reaction was abroad in the country. The United States in the ascending march of their free democracy have known more than one 16th of May. They had not been spared the swing of the pendulum and the return to power of the conservative party. The State of New York had at this time actually abolished the office of superintendent of schools which it had created several years previous. In Connecticut a political reaction had deprived Barnard of his position as superintendent. Why should not Massachusetts follow their example by suppressing its Board of Education? Religious animosities sought disguise under political pretexts. The Board, that product of freedom, was represented as a dangerous instrument of centralization, an organ of despotic authority opposed to the spirit of American institutions. In spite of all this agitation "the bigots," as Mann called them, were defeated by 245 to 182 votes. Does not this recall the doubtful victories which Jules Ferry won in 1880, when he barely obtained from the Senate by small majorities the vote for the school laws?

Mann had not only to struggle against religious fanaticism and to repel the assaults of the *odium theologicum*. To the orthodox sectarians were joined the defenders of routine and tradition in education. It was in 1843 and 1844 that the storm burst forth with peculiar violence, excited by the publication of Mann's report on his return from abroad, in which he set forth the pedagogical superiority of the Old World. The school-teachers of Boston, to the number of thirty-one, banded themselves against him. They had never forgiven him his appointment as secretary of the

Board of Education in place of a professional teacher. And now was it to be calmly endured that an American should remark, among many similar observations, that when he beheld the activity of masters and pupils in European schools, the schools of his own country seemed to him, in comparison, like dormitories, and the pupils like "hibernating animals — actual marmots"?

Accordingly, the Boston professors on the plea of patriotic sentiment proceeded to draw up a species of arraignment against the Board and its secretary. Their appeal was undoubtedly addressed to the national pride, wounded by the preference which Mann avowed for European schools, but at bottom it was tradition with all its array of prejudices which had risen against this innovator.

And it must be added that the professors in their campaign against Mann were joined by the authors and editors of classical school-books, who felt their interests threatened, and who resented statements like the following: "There are at this moment three hundred text-books in use where twenty or thirty would be sufficient." Teachers are, as a rule, conservative in spirit and opposed to innovations; those of Boston were peculiarly so, by reason of the exceptional position which their early fame had given them throughout the country. They were justly proud of their schools, of which it had been said that they were the "glory and pride of Massachusetts." Faithful to their traditions, and feeling that they had carried the time-honored system to perfection, they could not conceive of any change as desirable or any progress as possible. They had done very well without a board of education for two hundred years; they could do without it still. Mann had come with his bold undertakings, upsetting established institutions and disturbing time-honored customs. His free and ardent speech, his mind eager in quest of novelties, unsettled the general tranquillity, and what authority had he for so doing? He was a mere amateur philosopher, meddling in matters of education of which he knew nothing, without practical experience or scholastic antecedents, — a lawyer astray amid pedagogues! And while formulating their grievances, the one and thirty Boston pedagogues at the same time multiplied their accusations. Not one of the innovations attempted by Mann found favor in their eyes. Normal schools were useless, since there had always been a supply of good teachers without them. Have we not encountered similar opposition in France in 1880 and 1881 when the government of the Third Republic inaugurated the higher normal schools of Fontenay and Saint-Cloud? Mann replied that one of the essential duties of the State was to take efficacious measures to guarantee the professional education of schoolmasters. "The school committees," he said, "are like sentinels stationed at the door of every schoolhouse to make sure that only the best teachers whom it is possible to procure shall enter."

The new methods of discipline, as Mann understood it, were incriminated. The schoolmasters were of the same opinion as the theologian Smith: they regretted to see banished from the schools religion — and the lash!

Yet on this point Mann did not show himself intractable. He undoubtedly considered it the duty of masters to rule by reason and the heart, by arousing the highest sentiments and motives of action, but in extreme cases, where moral suasion proved insufficient, where the charms of knowledge and the interest of study were not enough to secure order and industry, he admitted, as did Locke, that recourse should be had to corporal punishment. These violent attacks of his adversaries acted injuriously upon Mann and irritated him to the point of affecting his health. It is at this period that he wrote to a physician, a friend of his: "Can you do anything for a patient who has not slept for three weeks? I feel an inextinguishable fire inside my brain, continually blazing, like the flame of dry wood blown by the wind."

Mann was undoubtedly kind and gentle by nature, and in the language of phrenology, which was so dear to him, he had the "bump" of benevolence highly developed. But on this occasion, stung to the quick by the unjust strictures of his opponents, he lost patience. Not content, in his replies, with defending himself, he attacks in his turn, and assumes the offensive with considerable temper and acrimony. He lashes the partisans of routine and does not spare insulting epithets. "There are owls," he cries, "who, to suit the universe to their blind eyes, would prevent the sun from rising."

Mann suffered therefore in this campaign which was being waged against him; but some good resulted to the cause which he was defending. Public opinion received a fresh impulse; attention was brought to bear upon the Boston public schools; the pupils were subjected to a public examination, and the defects in their instruction were pointed out. Henceforth, the masters stood alone in regarding them as perfect. It was shown, for example, that the practice of flogging as a punishment exceeded all bounds. To remedy this evil, the school committee ordered that in future a register of punishments should be kept under supervision. A short time after, Mann learned with satisfaction that corporal punishment had diminished twenty-five per cent.

But Mann's ardor was not directed merely toward reforming existing schools; it showed itself also in important new creations, notably in the establishment of normal schools. Mann is the actual founder of the United States normal schools, which to-day number one hundred and seventy-eight, public and private. He established three in Massachusetts. Henry Barnard followed his example in Connecticut in 1839. The State of New York in its turn founded that of Albany, whose first principal was the celebrated David Page. In Mann's eyes no other question equalled this in importance.

"I regard normal schools as a new instrument of progress for the improvement of the human race. I consider that without them the public schools would lose their strength and power for good and become mere charity schools. Neither the art of printing, nor freedom of the press, nor free suffrage could long subsist for useful and salutary ends if schools for the education of teachers ceased to exist. In fact, if we allow the character and talents of school-teachers to be lowered, the schools will become poor, and poor schools will form poor minds, and the free press will become a lying and licentious press, and the ignorant elector will become a venal elector until, under the outward form of a republic, a set of depraved and criminal men will govern the country."

In 1839 and 1840 three normal schools were founded at Mann's suggestion: one at Lexington for women teachers only, the two others at Barre and Bridgewater for both sexes.

Undertaken provisionally and as an experiment, they were only definitely established on the 2d of March, 1842, when the legislature voted an annual sum for their maintenance. It was a welcome day to Mann and was not without a morrow, since on the 3d of March the House voted a further grant for school libraries.

"Never," he wrote, "have brighter days dawned upon our cause. The delight which I feel at the success of our plans does not grow less and will have a salutary effect upon my health and spirits. The painful toil, which I have undergone for years, has been like a vampire sucking the blood from my heart and the marrow from my bones. I feel now that my strength will revive, and I shall be able to do more and better work."

Normal schools, however, had a very modest beginning in Massachusetts. In Lexington, on the opening day, only three young girls inscribed their names. The term of study was to be of one year only, as it was with us at the opening of Fontenay-aux-Roses. These new institutions did not lack critics; they were accused, in the first place, of drawing pupils away from the academies,—those colleges for intermediate instruction which up to this time had supplied with more or less success the men and women teachers for the primary schools. These critics refused to admit that popular education required for the professional training of its teachers special schools distinct from those where general culture was combined with a solid technical education. What wonder that the views of these opponents of the movement found credit among Mann's contemporaries, when in our own day we have witnessed advanced minds demanding the suppression of our one hundred and sixty normal schools, which are, nevertheless, among the finest orks of the Third Republic, and proposing to transfer the training of instructors to the Lycees and universities?

On the other hand, Mann found himself surrounded by enthusiastic adherents. Already in 1837 the Rev. Charles Brooks had accompanied him on his lecture tours and supported him in his campaign in behalf of the normal school with such ardent zeal that the opposition newspapers published caricatures in which Mr. Brooks was depicted as a coachman, whip in hand, driving a team of school-teachers toward a normal school in the clouds. . . .

The American normal school, however, descended from the clouds to the solid earth, thanks to the efforts of Mann and his friends, and also to the generosity of a good citizen, Mr. Edmund Dwight, who offered a donation of $10,000 toward the professional training of school masters and mistresses, on condition that the State should contribute a like sum. This method has since become a popular one among wealthy patrons of education in the United States. These benefactors are in the habit of offering one or two millions, or even more, for the founding of a university or library, provided that the government or other donors shall provide an equal sum; and this measure invariably succeeds, thereby justifying the familiar saying that it is only the first step that costs. Edmund Dwight was neither a Carnegie, a Rockefeller, nor a Leland Stanford. The America of 1838 had not yet witnessed those princely donations which in our day have sometimes exceeded a million dollars. Nevertheless, Mr. Dwight's gift of $10,000 caused deep joy, "indescribable joy," to Horace Mann.

Another and different form of good luck attended him in the foundation of his normal schools. He had the rare fortune to be able to lay his hand upon a number of distinguished men to start and direct them; among whom we may name Samuel Newman, Nicholas Tillinghast, and that incomparable educator, Cyrus Pierce. Mann discovered the latter during one of his tours of inspection in 1837 on the little island of Nantucket, where Pierce had for many years been conducting schools which Mann pronounced the best in Massachusetts, schools in which order and discipline were maintained solely by an appeal to the conscience of the scholars.

At the Lexington Normal School Pierce accomplished wonders. On September 14, 1845, Mann wrote in his private journal: "I have passed the whole day in Mr. Pierce's school, and a most agreeable day it was. I had already formed a high opinion of his talents, but he surpassed my expectations both in the art of teaching and in that gift which is the real condition of success in all instruction, — that of gaining the confidence of his pupils. I have seen nothing like it in any other school."

Pierce was a second Mann, with the same uprightness, the same lofty ideals, the same devotion to his work, in which he wore himself out. "Without him," wrote Barnard, "the cause of normal schools would have been lost for many years." At the close of each of his classes he repeated to his scholars: "Children, live for truth!" An old normal student of Lexington wrote: "The walls of our school have so often echoed these words that were they to crumble to pieces, we should still hear, sounding above the crash of their fall, "Live for truth!"

Mann used the same language: "There is no treasure comparable to truth; there is no such source of happiness as truth; there is no cure for misfortune like truth. . . ."

Another of Mann's important works was the formation of school libraries. He took the utmost pains to develop a taste for reading and to place good books within reach of all, even in the remotest villages. "There is at this day," he wrote, "only a seventh part of the population provided with opportunities for reading, while for the majority, who do not know how to read and have no means of obtaining books, it is actually as if printing had never been invented." His joy was therefore great when he obtained from the legislature in

1842, a grant for the purpose of purchasing books for each school district. He hailed this decision as an event of the utmost importance, second only to that act of 1647, by which public schools were founded by the State. The small sum of fifteen dollars was allotted to each community, which should subscribe an equal sum for the foundation or maintenance of a local library. In case the children of the district numbered twice or thrice the minimum of sixty, the sum was to be doubled or trebled. The school library, as Mann understood it, was to be open to parents as well as to children. "When the schoolhouse is well provided with books," he said, "grown men will again turn their steps thither." He wished them to be established everywhere, even in the smallest villages; "so that in future there shall not be a child without a collection of books at his disposal at all times, without cost, and within a half-hour's walk of his dwelling." He considered reading as powerful an agent in the world of mind as steam in the world of matter.

"Let a child read and understand the stories in which great virtues are set forth, such, for example, as the friendship of Damon and Pythias, the integrity of Aristides, the fidelity of Regulus, the stainless purity of Washington, the invincible perseverance of Franklin, and he will think and act differently for the rest of his life. Let a young man read a popular treatise on astronomy or geology, and henceforth new skies will arch above his head, a new earth will be spread beneath his feet."

Mann devoted himself with his habitual energy to the creation of libraries. To an already enormous correspondence he added thousands of letters, stimulating their formation in each of the three or four thousand schools in Massachusetts. He knew well, moreover, that it was not enough to have books, but that they must also be well chosen. Mann would have liked the Board of Education to draw up an official list of books which it approved. But as this proceeding of preliminary censure appeared illiberal and alarmed the book trade, Governor Morton refused to sanction it. Mann was therefore obliged to confine himself to persuasion and to indicating the books he preferred. He distrusted works of fiction and, what is more surprising, historical works. Doubtless, a nation as young as America, a nation almost without a history, has less need than others to study the past; but what indisposed Mann especially toward history was the complacency with which it recounts wars of conquest and sanguinary battles, and the robberies and rapacities of kings and emperors, with all the moral atrocities and abominations of an earlier time, which in his opinion were to be attributed rather to the ignorance than to the perversity of mankind. In order that history might be studied with profit by children, he would have it rewritten and in another spirit — "What a series of thefts and rapines is the history of the past!"

What, then, were the books recommended by him? They were all books useful to morals, such as biographies of great men, stories which tend to develop "courage and noble sentiments," as well as practical treatises on hygiene and popular science, "such as are suitable for active men in a poor country whose sterile soil needs science to render it fertile." Mann thought, with reason, that the people needed a new literature, and in order to embody his ideas, he negotiated with the booksellers of Boston to publish two series of books in cheap editions, one in 18mo for children, the other in 12mo for adults; and in preparing them, he called to his assistance the most competent writers of his time, such as Washington Irving, the novelist, Edward Everett, the moralist, George B. Emerson, and others. What he desired was a form of literature as simple as it was elevated, and especially adapted to the capacity of children.

"In most of the reading-books in use, one finds," he says, "moral aphorisms in which great thinkers have embodied their life-long experience and reflection; maxims in which philosophers have condensed the loftiest scientific truths; and these are offered as early lessons to children, as if, because they are born after Bacon and Franklin, they are at once capable of understanding them."

Mann's pedagogic work was immense, and we will not attempt to give an account here of all his reforms, of all the various measures which he carried out or participated in: including weekly lectures for teachers of both sexes; the creation in Boston of a model school which was to serve in the matter of architecture, furniture, books, methods, and masters as a pattern to all the others; the reunion in one central school of several small schools located in sparsely populated districts, for the benefit of the older scholars only, to whom the distance would be no obstacle; methods of obligatory instruction in vocal music and drawing; annual lectures to teachers to be given in each county during the vacations, a species of travelling normal school such as has always had a great vogue in the United States.

For the accomplishment of his purposes Mann did not neglect the most trifling means. In 1840 he conceived the idea of rekindling the zeal of the country districts by drawing up a set of tables, in which the Massachusetts towns were classified according to the importance of the sacrifices they had made for the support of public education. This graduated table, as he called it, was, he said himself, his stroke of genius. The publicity he gave to it aroused to an extraordinary degree the emulation of the various towns. In a similar manner, he sought to stimulate the zeal of the school committees, whose functions had hitherto been entirely gratuitous, by having a small indemnity assigned them, sufficient at least to defray their travelling expenses. Mann not only devoted his time and strength to the cause of education, he also expended for it a part of his emoluments as secretary, which consisted of about $1500, "a miserable salary," as it is called by Americans to-day. His disinterestedness and generosity equalled his zeal; nothing was awarded for the purchase of books, for his correspondence, or the expense of his lecture tours during four months of the year; he furnished at his own cost geographical maps to the schools; he likewise undertook his European trip at his own expense. No sacrifice was too great for the furtherance of his aim; pecuniary considerations appealed to him very slightly; he was astonished to find all his friends, with the exception of Channing, expressing curiosity as to the amount of the salary he received. In 1849 he announced that he made no claim to being indemnified for the expenses he incurred in the discharge of his duties. "From the day when I accepted the office of secretary," he said, "I considered myself responsible for the success of the undertaking, and were I to expend for it all my means, my health, my life, — nay, a hundred lives if I had them, — I should hold that the triumph of the cause far outweighed all these sacrifices."

But in spite of his protestations, a vote was passed allotting him an indemnity of $2000; George B. Emerson saying, "It has always seemed to me, that having made a great personal sacrifice in accepting the functions of secretary, Mann was less bound than any other citizen to contribute from his private purse to the success of the undertaking."

But this was what he was in the habit of doing, and what would he not have done to bring about the fulfilment of his dream, — he who had said from the beginning that he approached his task "in the spirit of martyrdom." The actual reward for him was in the results he had brought about, and which an American writer sums up in these words:

"During these twelve years of labor, the State aid granted to public schools was doubled; more than $2,000,000 were expended in improving the condition of school-houses; the salaries of teachers were raised 62 per cent for men and 51 per cent for women, while at the same time the number of women teachers was increased 54 per cent (3591 in 1837, 5510 in 1848); a month was added to the average duration of the school year; the proportion of private to public schools dwindled from 75 to 36 per cent; the supervision of the school committees became more general and more continuous; three normal schools were established, which sent out several hundreds of teachers, whose influence was to make itself felt in every part of the State."

Politics alternated with pedagogy in the varied career of Horace Mann. In 1848 a seat became vacant in the national Congress at Washington through the death of John Quincy Adams, former President of the United States, who was representative from Massachusetts. His succession was offered to Mann, who was elected by a large majority, his fellow-citizens thus showing their gratitude for the services he had rendered the State.

He accepted, abandoning his previous functions not without regret, but with the consciousness that as secretary of the Board of Education he had fulfilled his whole duty; that the impulse had been given; that education was advancing with rapid strides; and that, in short, the work being almost accomplished, he could henceforth be spared.

In 1861 he was reelected—a great triumph, in view of the violent campaign directed against him by the champions of slavery and sustained by the great authority of Daniel Webster, then Secretary of State. Mann had distinguished himself in the debates in Congress by his eloquence and zeal in behalf of all measures tending toward the abolition of slavery.[1] He had fought against its further extension, expressing himself in these words: "Rather than suffer it to invade other States, I should prefer the rupture of the Union, civil war, even servile war."

The four years during which Mann sat in Congress, always active and always eloquent, may be counted among the most brilliant pages in his career; but they are beside our subject, and we must now

---

[1] In a debate which lasted twenty-one days, he defended three abolitionists who had carried away fifty slaves in order to liberate them. He ended by obtaining the acquittal of his clients. See *Speeches on Slavery*, 1852.

return to the pedagogue who, four years later, reverted to his chosen mission and voluntarily assumed the presidency of Antioch College, there to display the qualities of an admirable, practical educator.

III

Horace Mann's Philosophy

Let us pause in the narrative of Mann's life and educational work — as he himself paused during the four years of his political life — and attempt to define briefly those principles and general ideas which constantly guided his efforts.

A man of action before all, a nature swayed by inspiration rather than reflection, Mann had not the leisure and lacked, moreover, the power of abstraction necessary for constructing a philosophy of his own. In his agitated and feverish life he found no time to condense his thoughts or to write learned treatises. Undoubtedly he wrote a great deal, as he spoke a great deal, but all his writings, whether reports, lectures, or speeches, — we were about to say sermons, — were primarily action, and bore the stamp of the orator. He had no personal philosophy beyond an ardent faith in progress and the indefinite perfectibility of the human race. The critical spirit is not that which generally distinguishes American thinkers. The spirit of analysis, moreover, is rarely allied with enthusiasm, and enthusiasm was the dominant note in Mann's intelligence. Let us not ask from him, therefore, a coordinate whole, a system of clear and precise views upon human nature. His psychology remained always confused and inexact. It sets out with a confession of impotence: "The nature of mind is impenetrable." Mann accepts the most daring theories; as, for example, that liberty consists of one thing only, — the choice between good and evil. The choice made once for all between obedience or disobedience to the divine law, "the law seizes us and flings us high or low, raises us or lowers us with irresistible power." In other words, one moment — one only — of freedom is granted us, then we bow beneath the yoke of a kind of fatality. This is to simplify too much, and to solve somewhat lightly, the problem of the complex play of human will and action.

Where Mann was not mistaken was in affirming that there are laws, — without, however, knowing precisely what they are, — laws presiding over the formation of minds as imperious as those which preside over the production of flowers and fruits. And Mann understood thoroughly that it was necessary to know these laws in order to establish solidly the foundations of education. He knew that pedagogy must rest on a philosophical doctrine. "How can we conduct education," he said, "without having conceived a theory of the mind?" Not being able to frame for himself this theory which he sought, he borrowed it. He found in his path, so to speak, the philosophy of an English writer, George Combe, and adopted it; he made it his own, somewhat as the spiritualistic philosopher Boyer-Collard, according to Laine, having found and purchased one day at a book-stall on the quays of the Seine, the works of the Scotchman Thomas Reid, founded thereon the official French philosophy of the nineteenth century.

Who was George Combe? A man of heart assuredly, who merited the sympathy of his great friend in America. They had made each other's acquaintance in Boston, whither Combe had gone in 1838 to deliver a course of lectures. Mann heard him and was won over at once to his views. They formed a close friendship which was severed only by death and was kept alive by an active correspondence. Combe said of Mann: "He was a delightful companion and friend; of all the men I met in Boston, he was the best." While Mann, on his side, wrote to Combe: "There is no man of whom I think oftener than of you, or who has done me so much good as you."

Combe had published in 1828 a volume entitled *The Constitution of Man*. Mann speaks of it with extraordinary enthusiasm and some naïvete. He regards it as a "masterpiece of thought." Combe's philosophy seems to him destined to work in the moral sciences a revolution analogous to that of Bacon in the domain of physical science; and carrying hyperbole to its utmost limits, he exclaims: "Just as there could be but one discovery of the circulation of the blood, or of the solar system, so there could be but one author of *The Constitution of Man*." [1]

George Combe hardly merited such emphatic eulogiums. His doctrine was, after all, but a poor and mediocre philosophy, in which the author developed in a cold and prosaic style the narrow, meagre psychological system of Gall and the phrenologists. It is easy, however, to account for Mann's genuine devotion to the ideas of the English psychologist. There was a certain intellectual affinity between them. Combe was not one of those con-

---

[1] George Combe published in 1840 another work which also aroused Mann's admiration: "Your *Moral Philosophy* is worthy of your *Constitution of Man*, without being equal to it, which would be impossible." Mann's sincerity is proved by the fact that he could speak disagreeable truths to his friend, as, for example, on his publishing a *Journal of Education* which Mann thought unworthy of him.

templative philosophers who confine themselves to the region of pure speculation; he presented his psychology rather as an introduction to the science and art of education; hence his essays in the region of a higher and more analytical philosophy adapt themselves admirably to the instructive views of Mann. He was also a friend to popular education; and his writings on pedagogy were not devoid of merit, since twenty years after his death they were still held in honor among his countrymen. That which chiefly attracted Mann in his system must have been, first, his attempts to frame national moral laws for the government of mankind, — laws to which it was only necessary to conform to attain wisdom; and, secondly, his recommendation of care of the body no less than of the mind. In his system physical health was a condition of the soul's health, a principle of morality; proper food and clothing being, according to his view, as essential elements in the happiness of mankind as books and lessons. The question of alimentation had always been of the highest importance in Mann's estimation. "It is a great misfortune," he said, "that the quantity and quality of food which a people consume cannot be determined by some fixed rule;" and elsewhere: "As I grow older and, I hope, wiser, I am conscious that the contempt I formerly professed for the stomach and the lungs has gradually changed into a sort of respect for these bodily organs. They are not *Dii majores*, but *Dii minores*, without whose aid the higher faculties of the brain are as disabled as a sea-captain would be who attempted to navigate his ship without sailors."

There was nothing in Combe's system, even to its fundamental idea of the cerebral localization of the various faculties of the mind, but was of a nature to attract Mann.[1] Freed from what savors of charlatanism, such as the claim that the bumps on the cranium are the outward manifestation of mental qualities phrenology contains a kernel of truth which partly justifies the success it obtained with Mann and his friend.[2] It teaches that the human faculties are so many distinct forces which can be developed by exercise, by an appropriate activity. This is what Mann never ceased to repeat, being convinced in advance of

---

[1] Mann is not the only distinguished man over whom G. Combe exerted an influence. Mr. John Morley has shown in one of his books, *The Life of Richard Cobden*, that the illustrious economist had also been influenced by him (1881).

[2] Phrenology was the fashion in America at this time. Nearly all Mann's friends, Pierce, George B. Emerson, Dr. Howe, were fervent adherents of it.

a doctrine which places man's destiny in his own hands, so to speak, and proclaims the omnipotence of education, since it is able to insure and regulate the development of all the faculties by means of the activity it imparts to them.

When Mann essayed himself, following Combe, to define what he calls "the laws of the mind," "the laws of God," he indicated but two such laws, which, according to him, should be the guides of the human mind.

The first is the law of symmetry, which demands that all our faculties should be developed in harmony and with perfect balance, each of them growing stronger through the support of the others. Hitherto, nations, like individuals, have exaggerated certain qualities at the expense of others; thus the perfectly well-balanced man is nowhere to be found.

The second law is that our faculties are strengthened by exercise and perish from inaction. "How many forces are suffered to lie dormant which gradually become extinct; on the other hand, how many benefits and miracles might be wrought for mankind by prolonged exercise and continuous effort! Witness Franklin, the good and great Franklin." Mann had early severed his connection with all religious bodies to become an adherent of natural religion only.[1] He was a Puritan in some respects, but a Puritan without theology.

He complained that natural religion was not understood in his day, nor its power appreciated. "It is," he affirmed, "as superior to revealed religion as a personal experience is to a vague hearsay." He doubtless recognized the elevating influence which established religions have exercised in the past, "in guiding generations of mankind through the darkness of the world;" but he hoped for and desired the speedy coming of a religion founded upon reason, freed from outworn dogmas and impenetrable mysteries. "The hour has come when the light of natural religion shall be to that of revealed religion what the blaze of the rising sun is to the pale gleam of the stars."

He was religious, then, profoundly religious; a vague mysticism floats over expressions like these: "Soul speaks to soul, words and even thoughts are merely accessory." Or again: "The spiritual essence of man contemplates directly the spiritual essence of the universe." But from this religious spirit all dogma, all formal *Credo*, is

[1] Let us add, however, that he often spoke as a Christian, in a spirit of worship or at least of reverence for Christ. He said before his death to his wife and children: "If ever you are perplexed as to what you ought to do, ask yourselves what Jesus Christ would have done in your place."

banished. Belief in an all-powerful creator, in a God of goodness, and in an immortality of happiness alone survive in his religion.

The immortality of the soul was for Mann an undisputed article of faith, but he looked upon it from the point of view of the infinite joy reserved for the elect. In his writings, in his discourses, he unceasingly evokes the idea of the future life, not only with hope, but with certainty; and although he scarcely believed in school rewards, — any more than in punishments, — he believed firmly in the rewards of another life and desired a heaven for all.

"Why have not all men entered this life virtuous, to be transported as by a lightning flash to the felicity of the next?" "We must know how to bear suffering, to submit without comprehending it in expectation of the compensations of eternity. The divine law is eternal; it follows us in this world and the next, making of the two but one world, and reducing death simply to an incident of life. Our virtuous and criminal actions will live always in their good and evil consequences: how much more, then, shall the agent himself live!"

And with the emphasis habitual to his eloquence he adds: —

"A grain of wheat buried with the mummy of Sesostris may germinate anew to-day and unite the nineteenth century with the remotest antiquity. Can, then, the soul of the great king be dissolved into nothingness?"

We have said that Mann's psychology is uncertain and vague. He has, nevertheless, attempted to sketch in broad outlines this psychology, which is rather a system of morality.

It is, in fact, the moral consciousness and the sense of responsibility which Mann places in the first rank among the higher faculties of man. Immediately after these, he places — even before the family affections — the social and sympathetic faculties, benevolence toward others, philanthropy. In other words, man is above all a creature of duty, subject to moral law; in the next place, he is a being devoted to others. Mann neither sought nor found the opportunity for becoming a martyr, but in another age he would have been capable of it in the service of humanity or to attest his social faith.

"The history of the heroes of antiquity and of the martyrs of Christianity, although their dust has been scattered for centuries, arouses in us such transports of admiration that we long to be in their place; and this passion raises us to such heights that the most terrible death for a sacred cause appears to us as lovely and desirable as the young bride to her bridegroom."

And after exalting these high and noble aspirations of human nature, Mann brands with pitiless sternness the egotistic sentiments, the lower propensities, which make of man, when they rule him, "a ferocious beast, a bird of prey." "Neither in the den of the lion nor in the vulture's eyry do there exist brigands comparable to those men who are dominated by the insatiable appetites of selfishness."

Intelligence, strictly so called, the intelligence which reasons, which analyzes, which decides dryly and coldly, is not Mann's affair. He deliberately subordinates the reasoning being to the being of sentiment; and it is precisely here that we must seek the secret of his strength, of the sovereign power which his inspired eloquence exerted over his contemporaries. / He was, above all, a man of heart, — one who surrendered himself to the instincts of a noble nature, who felt before thinking, and whose sentiments, brimful of the sap of spring, overflowed and bloomed with life, youth, and freshness. How wide is the gulf between this sensitive soul, sentimental, even quick, to enthusiastic beliefs, faithful without reserve to the fundamental principles of human nature, and the "Intellectuals" of our day, whose destructive criticism would shatter, if we listened to them, our faith in humanity and its eternal aspirations! How he would have suffered, how startled as well as wounded his conscience would have been, could he have known to what a frenzy of negation an abuse of the analytic spirit was to lead some of the men who followed him!

We analyze to-day the idea of patriotism, and it melts away to give place to the chimera of internationalism; we analyze the idea of property, and it is reduced to collectivism; we analyze the idea of God and are led to atheism; we analyze the idea of the family, and behold indifferent and ungrateful sons; we analyze the idea of duty, and the moral law becomes a mere word devoid of meaning.

Amid these divagations of an overstimulated intellectualism, Mann would have appealed more forcibly than ever to the primal instincts of nature in defence of things sacred in his eyes. He would have reiterated that the ideal of the thinker is to combine with the light of pure thought that ardor and warmth of sentiment which are also, in themselves, a light.

"If the best wines are those for which the grapes have ripened on the slopes of a volcano, so the best thoughts are those that spring from a clear brain warmed by a large heart." Mann always subordinated intellectual to moral culture. In one of his reports he wrote: —

"How many lessons, recitations, and examinations we require for the development of the mind! What a multitude of books must be read and reread! But for the formation of character and right feeling, what poverty of instruction! What do we teach children in regard to their reciprocal duties, the affection which brothers and sisters owe each other? What as to filial piety, as to the obligations of men of wealth toward those less fortunate than themselves? How do we teach them to avoid the passions of pride and greed, of envy and revenge? What as to the countless calamities resulting from drink and gambling? Does arithmetic teach them the folly of investing in lotteries? Does history insist strongly enough upon the criminal character of nine-tenths of the wars it records, and upon the horrible sufferings they have brought upon the human race? When teaching of such importance as this is neglected, children may indeed become good grammarians and ready reckoners, but will they be just, good, and benevolent men?"

Thus Mann's pedagogy, like his psychology, consisted chiefly of morality. "He who does the most good to his fellow-men," he said, "is the master of masters and has learned the art of arts."

Mann's countrymen have often called him a radical, even a revolutionary; to us he appears, on the contrary, to have been a wise and prudent spirit, a moderate opportunist in every respect, except in his speech, which was overemphatic and at times slightly declamatory. He knew how to make necessary concessions and to accept compromises. He understood that by violently attacking tradition and established customs one runs the risk of losing everything. If, in the last years of his life, he joined an organized church, it was because he regarded this step as useful to his designs and necessary to the success of the cause of which he had constituted himself the champion; the Christian Union, of which he became a member, being the only door open to liberal ideas in the West.

Mann had had no regular teachers before the age of twenty; he had been, above all, the pupil of nature. We might assume that an education of this sort, a chance education, as it were, would have left something disorderly in his mind; but it was not so. Aside from certain flights of the imagination, Mann's is a classic mind. His taste for lofty language, the large and ample construction of his speeches, reveal what we might call a spontaneous classic culture. He had a special taste for the Latin authors and quotes them as constantly as a humanist might do. He tells us that in his youth, if he chanced to meet a young girl who was a Latin scholar, he regarded her as a sort of divinity.

Nevertheless, the utilitarian and practical tendencies, suitable to a good American, reveal themselves in the spirit of this humanist. "What satisfactory argument can we invoke," he asks, "to show why algebra, a science which not one man in a thousand has occasion to use in the affairs of life, should be studied by more than 2300 scholars in the Massachusetts schools, whereas bookkeeping, which all, even workmen, require, is only taught to about half that number?[1] For farmers and road-makers, why give geometry the preference over land-surveying? And why, among those who devote themselves to the pursuit of intellectual truth, are the students of rhetoric twice as numerous as those of logic?"

No one has expressed more forcibly the law of solidarity, which unites successive generations one to the other, and makes universal education

---

[1] At Antioch Mann struggled for months to obtain the appointment of a professor of bookkeeping.

a debt which the nation must discharge by assuming the whole expense of maintaining schools. This idea he formulates in three propositions: —

"1. Successive generations of mankind taken collectively constitute one great community.

"2. All the wealth which this community possesses it owes to all its children with a view to providing them with an education adequate to protect them from poverty and vice, and prepare them worthily to perform their civic and social duties.

"3. The successive holders of this wealth are merely its trustees, bound by the most sacred obligations to execute their mandate faithfully; and to divert this wealth from its true object, the education of the young, is as great a crime, indeed a greater one, than similar breach of faith with contemporaries."

Convinced, as he was, of the necessity of education, Mann seems to have hesitated for a time in regard to the question of compulsory school attendance. He was not by nature inclined toward restraint or the rigor of any law whatever, but, on the contrary, expected everything from the charms which enlightenment must have for souls plunged in the darkness of ignorance.

"Let the intelligent man," he said, "visit the ignorant daily, as the oculist visits the blind and removes the scales from their eyes until the living sense opens once more to the living light. Let the zealous man enter into communion with those torpid from indifference, and melt the ice in which they are entombed. Let the love of childhood, the love of country, the dictates of reason, the sentiment of religious responsibility, unite in a wise blending of tenderness and severity, until the grim, hard mass of ignorance, avarice, and prejudice gives way before the combined action of their heat and light."

Let us wait, in other words, until the people desire education before offering it to them. But is it not a mistake to let oneself be misled by the illusions of a chimerical optimism? Does not history prove that in order that a people shall seek instruction, they must be forced to it? Mann, in fact, speedily renounced his error; by the year 1847 he had completely changed his opinion, and warned by experience of the indifference and carelessness of parents, he recognized the need for enforcing school attendance.

Mann was not merely a powerful orator whose heart animated his voice and kindled his accents, and whose broad mind overflowed with ideas: he was also a skilled and persuasive writer. It has been said of his style that it was as brilliant and flowery as spring in a New England meadow. It was even too much so, perhaps. His ardent imagination not only inspired him with prophetic visions, great conceptions of the future: it also enriched his thought and style with an excessive wealth of imagery.

He himself acknowledged — and it was a defect in his own eyes — "the profusion and redundance of his metaphors." And he added gracefully: "This fault would perhaps be forgiven me if one knew what trouble I daily take to refuse to my tongue and pen the flood of metaphors which invade my imagination." We can the more easily forgive him this poetic exuberance in consideration of its having greatly contributed to the success of his undertakings. He neither wrote nor spoke for the learned and literary; he addressed popular audiences; and he was forced, in order to be understood, to multiply his arguments and develop his ideas somewhat diffusely. He was obliged, in order that he might dominate the minds of his readers and hearers, to be prodigal of metaphors and figures of speech. How many brilliant pages we could quote, were it not that their force would be weakened, their brilliancy dimmed, by the attempt to condense them! None of the great ideas which constitute the modern spirits were unknown to Mann, and he expressed them with equal vigor and poetic feeling. Of science, he says that it invests us with a sort of creative power, and that "man's dominion over the earth spreads in proportion to his knowledge." Of the beauty of nature, he says that she opened up to us a world of marvels: "Dazzling flowers on the great lap of earth, colored star rays in the infinite azure of the skies, brilliant tints of the young foliage, still more brilliant hues of the dying foliage in autumn." And above the true and the beautiful, above the world of true thoughts and beautiful things, he shows us what he calls the sublimity of the moral world.

"The laws of physical nature are sublime, but there exists a moral sublimity, before which the highest intelligence bows down and adores. The laws which cause the winds to blow, the tides to rise and fall, planets to roll, and suns to shine, the laws which preside over the subtle combinations of atoms and the terrible speed of electricity, the laws of germination and reproduction in the vegetable and animal kingdom, whatever be their radiant beauty, pale and fade before the moral glories which envelop the universe in celestial light. The heart is aware of charms which no beauty of things known, no dream of things unknown, can equal. Virtue shines with a purer ray than the diamond, the gardens of Arabia do not breathe so sweet a perfume as that of charity. . . ."

What a beautiful picture he draws of the honest man and good citizen! The purity of morals, the punctuality, probity, devotion to others, the spirit of self-sacrifice, of solidarity,— all these virtues he draws with a glowing pen. "The honest man, the good citizen, is doubtless not insensible to the charm of the arts, but he knows that the most beautiful of arts is to paint smiles and joy upon the pale cheeks of poor and suffering childhood." Reason and conscience have taught him "that it is not permissible to adorn rich galleries with the marvels of art while the orphan is neglected in the streets, while the sons of the intemperate and profligate have no school but that of obscenity and blasphemy, while the world is afflicted with infinite evils which superfluous wealth and wasted time would amply suffice to remedy."

Mann was a republican by conviction; he hailed with joy the rise of democracy without disguising from himself its dangers.

"I rejoice that power has passed irrevocably into the hands of the people. For ages upon ages humanity has groaned beneath oppression; whole races have been enslaved for the benefit of a chosen few. To gratify the ambition of tyrants, nations have perished on the battle-field. The noblest faculties of man have been obscured and crushed by ignorance and superstition. There has been an end to liberty of conscience, of thought, and of speech. Heaven itself has been offered for sale, like a piece of property, by men who had no right to it. . . . Power has now passed from the few to the many, from the oppressors to their victims. The rich, the noble, the privileged classes, had been granted authority for the benefit of the people and had misused it. Their fate is to-day in the hands of the people: its poverty commands their opulence; its ignorance decides their rights; its appetites threaten their homes. It is no longer a question of philanthropy with them; they have nothing to consider now but how to protect and save themselves. They will understand at last that the favored classes are safe only through the devotion or self-interest of the rest. . . ."

An optimist, like all good men who naturally incline to believe in the goodness of others and who, being sure of the nobility of their intentions, never dream of being misunderstood; and unable, like all active men, to imagine that their efforts will be in vain, Mann conceived high hopes for the future of humanity; but he was at the same time clear-sighted enough to perceive to what dangers the sovereign power of universal suffrage exposes a free democracy, if it is not enlightened by instruction and education; and of these fatal consequences of liberty in ignorance, he traced the darkest picture: —

"Already sounds on our ears the tread of that innumerable army of the coming generations. They are men who will take counsel only of their desires, which they will transform into laws; society will no longer be anything but the incarnation of their will, and if we take no more care than we have hitherto done to enlighten and regulate that will, it will engrave its laws upon the whole circuit of the globe in gigantic and awful characters."

Certainly he did not doubt the future of the republic nor its perpetuity.

"It would be easier to turn back the sun in his course than to monopolize again in the hands of a few the power which has passed into the hands of the people. Sooner will the oak reenter the acorn than we shall return to the monarchical and aristocratic forms of the past."

And elsewhere:

"Ideas of liberty, duty, and fraternity now move the nations, and neither the Pope with his

Cardinals nor the Czar with his Cossacks will succeed in suppressing them."

But to this triumphant democracy he gave the wisest counsels, and at all times and in all countries it is useful to hear and ponder his eloquent warnings; such, for example, as these: "It is perhaps easy to found a republic; it certainly is not easy to make republicans. Woe to the republic which is founded only upon the suffrage of ignorance, egotism, and passion! National representation is the faithful mirror of the mind and ideals of the people, and if these ideals are not on a level with its institutions, what perils and disasters are possible!"

Thus he reasoned more and more strongly for the necessity of universal education. "He is not an American statesman," he said, "who does not devote all his efforts to the education of the people." And this is equally true of every country on earth.

"Education is our only political safeguard; outside of this ark there is no salvation." If education did not succeed in preserving the public mind from corruption, all would be lost; all attempts to protect by law the property, the liberty, even the life of the citizen would be as vain as "the attempt to drive hornets from our orchards by means of sign-posts and warnings."

IV

Horace Mann, President of Antioch College

(1853–1859)

The interest never languishes in the life of Horace Mann; scarcely has he accomplished one task before he undertakes another. Men of action, such as he, never cease their activity in widely different directions; they labor till the last breath and die at their task.

The 15th of September, 1852, Horace Mann, member of Congress, was elected governor of Massachusetts by the free suffrage of his fellow-citizens. On the same day a society of friends of education offered him the presidency of a new college about to be established at Yellow Springs, Ohio. Called upon to choose between these two positions, Mann did not hesitate; he decided in favor of the more modest office, but the greater in his eyes, the academic one. This time he sacrificed politics to education.

He held the presidency of Antioch College for six years, until his death. It was a laborious and painful period of his life and in some respects a dramatic one. While this position offered a great field for his executive powers and revealed his rare gifts as a practical educator, it obliged him to contend with difficulties of every description; he suffered much as Pestalozzi had suffered at Yverdon, so that these last years of his life present at times a painful and pathetic spectacle.

The work to be undertaken was an interesting one and of a nature to tempt Mann's ambition. To his ardent imagination it appeared as an opportunity to regenerate the Western States, which were still partly wilderness and at least backward in order and civilization. It seemed to him that he had but to open in this new region a college for advanced study and lofty ethics, in order to import thither all the civilization which had long flourished in the more favored soil of the East. "Shall the West," he asked, "that empire as vast almost as that of the Cæsars, belong to science, virtue, and human brotherhood, or shall it become the prey of corruption and license? . . . It can only be civilized if a son of Massachusetts transplants there the spirit of the original States of the Union, — those States which have long reverenced religion and learning."

The spirit which was to preside, according to the plan of its founders, over this new institution was in perfect harmony with Mann's general views. At a preparatory gathering, the first Faculty Meeting held at his house in West Newton, in October, 1852, where the programme of studies was drawn up, he discovered, with delight, that they were in complete agreement. "We are all teetotalers," he wrote, "all anti-tobacco men, all anti-slavery men, and the majority are adepts in phrenology; all hostile to emulation, that is, opposed to any system of discipline founded on rewards and prizes, and which, by exciting children to compare themselves with their companions, leads them away from the true motive of action, which is to compare oneself with an ideal of excellence."

The agreement was equally close in religious matters; the promoters of the enterprise, though professing themselves free from all sectarian spirit, yet belonged, most of them, to a new association calling itself the Christian Union; they claimed to have no other creed than the Bible and to have cast aside all denominational bonds. They wished to be simply Christians after the manner of the first Christians in the city of Antioch, and it was for this reason that the college was named Antioch College. In 1853 Mann was already fifty-seven years of age; he had never, up to this time, been a practical instructor, or even done any regular teaching. It was thus a fortunate new departure for him to be able to devote the evening of his beautiful life to the application of his favorite ideas. Certainly it was not without regret that he left New England, the scene of his long scholastic propaganda and of his political career; and when he bade a last farewell to the friends who came to see him off, the strong man wept like a child. Moreover, he was not unaware, though he did not foresee them all, of the difficulties awaiting him in a comparatively rude region, so far behind that which he was leaving in traditions, morals, and social culture. These difficulties other educators had encountered before him, and he had been fully warned.

Twenty years earlier Catherine Beecher and her sister Harriet, the same who later, as Mrs. Harriet Beecher Stowe, became famous as the writer of *Uncle Tom's Cabin,* had met with hostility and opposition in undertaking to found a girls' college at Cincinnati. Three years before the foundation of Antioch, in 1850, Calvin Stowe, the husband of Harriet, a professor in Cincinnati, had been persecuted and driven out of the city by the partisans of slavery and forced to seek refuge in the East with his wife and family. Mann mentions in one of his letters that Catherine Beecher, as the result of her own experience, endeavored to dissuade him from his project by representing to him the obstacles he must encounter in the inhospitable region of the West. But it was all in vain, his mind was made up; his enthusiasm overflowed; and he exclaimed not without a touch of declamation: —

"Where the capital of the United States ought to be situated is here in the Mississippi Valley, which is to be the seat of its empire. No other valley, not the Danube, the Ganges, the Nile, nor the Amazon, is destined to exert so potent an influence over the future of humanity; and this is the reason why, if its people study the laws of God on social questions and strive to conform to them, they should rise to the contemplation of the future and enduring reign of beneficence and peace."

\ Antioch College opened its doors on the 5th of October, 1853, with nearly two hundred students. Over three thousand people assembled for the inaugural exercises. Mann pronounced a glowing oration, in which he gave utterance to his hope of conquering the West by education. "There is life enough in your Inaugural," wrote his friend, Theodore Parker, "to make a college flourish in the desert of Sahara." "To form young minds and hearts," he himself said, — "was not this the most beautiful task ever confided to a man or an angel?"

The reality failed to correspond with these bright visions. First came the annoyances attendant on moving into unfinished buildings. Antioch College, when Mann arrived there with his family, presented a forlorn spectacle: nothing was completed, all was still chaos or at most "arrested creation, on the third day." It required many months before the toil of building and moving was concluded. Unquestionably, the site was well chosen, — in the midst of a smiling landscape surrounded by verdure and tranquillity. The small town of Yellow Springs was famed, as its name indicates, for its springs of medicinal water; Mann was about to create fresh springs of moral life there.

To make room for the college buildings, they had been obliged to clear a forest. Huge stumps of trees were lying about in all directions upon the miry soil, which resembled a swamp.

Doubtless, private enterprises are admirable in their way, and we know that their tradition is happily preserved in the United States. But it must be acknowledged that such enterprises are not always carried out with the same precision and thoroughness as the State institutions of more centralized countries. Antioch had been supposed to have an endowment of $600,000,000, but the actual amount was not forthcoming, and the establishment opened with a deficit.

For several months extreme disorder reigned there; the hastily erected buildings were not enclosed by any wall or even fence, and the animals of the neighborhood entered the college precincts with the utmost freedom, — the famous Ohio pigs circulating through the corridors and often obstructing the way for masters and pupils. As there was no drinking water on the place, the young girls belonging to the college were obliged to fill their pitchers at a well a quarter of a mile distant, and this in the depth of winter and often in the snow. There were no fires to warm the buildings, and several cold months passed before the arrival of the furnaces which had been ordered. The interior furnishing was deficient not only in the comforts, but in the necessities of life: the library was devoid of books, there was a total absence of writing tables, so that the students were obliged to eat and study by turns at the same tables.

Some one has said: "Give us *men*, and it will matter little if we set up a university or a college in barracks, or the students live in tents!" Horace Mann was assuredly a *man*, but even his strong will could not supply the material deficiencies from which his colleagues and pupils were suffering. The students, ill-clothed and ill-fed, began to be insubordinate, and during the first year Mann feared that a mutiny might break out in the dining room, and by way of precaution he took his meals at the common table. The masters were not regularly paid, and it was found necessary to reduce the salaries and employ less expensive teachers. For a year and a half Mann did not touch his salary, but with a devotion to his task worthy of a Pestalozzi, he exclaimed: "I am ready to suffer anything for these young people!"

These difficulties were not confined to the first days; the situation grew worse and worse, and Mann experienced hours of profound discouragement. Not only did he behold the institution on the verge of financial ruin, but he was conscious of an ill-concealed opposition among those about him. The patrons of the enterprise, members of the Christian Union, claimed to belong to no sect, but at heart they inclined toward orthodoxy, and Mann's liberalism caused them some anxiety. When he decided to enter the pulpit and constitute himself a minister, there arose a fresh series of attacks against this improvised "clergyman." On the one hand, he was charged with having renounced his liberal convictions; on the other, with not having conformed to the laws of evangelical ordination.

Mann, as president of the college, was concerned merely with the moral direction of the house; he had no administrative duties and had not even the right to select his own professors. A superintendent had been appointed as his colleague, charged with the administration, who soon gave evidence, in his relations with Mann, of an unaccommodating temper, and who, instead of supporting his authority, constantly sought to undermine it — a second Schmid for this new Pestalozzi. Antioch also sustained attacks from those who had been on its staff, a pamphlet of over three hundred pages, criticising Mann and the college, having been circulated by a former professor who had been dismissed.

Finally, Mann was growing old; his strength was failing day by day. In 1855 he was attacked by a partial paralysis of the tongue and was confined for weeks to a bed of suffering. But his iron will was stronger than disease, stronger than the hostility of his enemies. "Here I am, and here I stay," he wrote; "I try to think the sunrises and sunsets as beautiful as those I gazed upon in Boston in the society of my friends." Nothing could turn him aside from his great mission as an educator, which comprised two things, inseparable in his eyes, — to honor God and serve humanity. "We must succeed or die," he wrote. He succeeded, indeed, in a great measure, and he died at his task!

Mann's first concern had been to organize the course of study, and this could not be regularly accomplished for some time. The students who poured into Antioch College at its opening were not ordinary students nor easily classified; they were of all ages and all conditions, — adolescents, adults, and even married men. Attracted by Mann's great reputation, a number of ministers had abandoned their parishes in order to follow a college course. But all, or nearly all, were of such exceptional ignorance that the professors were driven to their wits' ends. Out of the total number of pupils admitted in 1853 — about two hundred — seven only were found capable of constituting a small freshman class; that is to say, of entering on a first year of secondary studies.

All this, it is true, changed rapidly; and to the disorderly rabble of the first days there succeeded in the following years a carefully culled elite. The college was no longer open to the first comer; applications had grown so numerous that Mann was able to discriminate; he accordingly established entrance examinations with rigid conditions of admission. And herein is clearly shown the character of an educator who valued moral qualities above intellectual gifts: out of all the young men who presented themselves, Mann made a selection based on moral rather than intellectual qualifications; the highest knowledge in his opinion being reserved as the privilege of virtuous youth.

He reversed the terms of the Socratic adage, "He who is wise is good," and said, "Only he who is good shall be called to become wise." This was to overlook the necessity for educating all; it was also to simplify the problem of moral education by well-nigh suppressing it altogether. In order to secure beforehand the moral integrity of his college, Mann sought to admit to it only worthy young men. He closed its doors to all whose characters did not seem to him to offer a sufficient guarantee for the future. He put them on their trial, so to speak, during the preparatory course of three years, to which he admitted all applicants on condition of eliminating, as soon as it became necessary, the incorrigibly vicious. And he admitted to the benefits of the higher education what he called "the privileges and delights of science and letters" — only those youths whose morals and character he had proved.

Under these conditions, with a carefully selected body of students under such a leader as Mann, Antioch could not fail to become a model college. The system of instruction was founded, on the whole, upon the pattern of the older New England colleges; Latin and Greek were taught, and the degree of B.A. was conferred upon graduates. Mann, however, introduced some interesting innovations into his course of studies. He gave a larger place to the sciences and history, in spite of his prejudice against the latter study, and inscribed physiology and hygiene on a college course for the first time. Always concerned with the problem of training efficient teachers, he founded courses on the theory and practice of teaching, thus making of Antioch a sort of normal school.

But it was in his methods, above all, that Mann introduced innovations: first, by establishing the system of optional courses, those "electives" which still enjoy such favor in the United States and which the reforms of 1902 have partially introduced into French secondary education. He made it obligatory to follow all the courses in the senior class only, where particular attention was paid to historical and philosophical studies. Another novelty was the preference given to oral instruction over teaching by books. "The fewest text-books possible" was Mann's motto. The cultivation of speech was one of his hobbies, and he wished that even children should have daily practice in describing the objects about them and in relating a story orally.

It is evident that Mann had reflected seriously upon questions of practical pedagogy. In his inaugural address on assuming the presidency of Antioch, he discussed several of these essential problems; as, for instance: Is it from the humanities and the dead languages or from mathematics and the natural sciences that we should seek the true discipline of the mind? How can science be reconciled with literature in a plan of studies and how is specialization to be combined with general culture? How can the professor who is himself a seeker for truth develop the love of research in his pupils?

Mann was not content merely to direct and inspire the teaching of his colleagues: he himself taught the branches of moral philosophy and political economy, thus reserving as his part the training of the honest man and good citizen. He occupied, moreover, the chair of natural theology; and in these various directions he was, according to the testimony of his pupils, an accomplished teacher. His teaching was "stimulating and suggestive," we are told, and there was something in it of feminine delicacy and gentleness.

But it was especially in the house discipline, of which all the responsibility rested on him, that Mann showed his originality. It was a discipline of freedom, by which the students were taught to guide themselves; supervision was dispensed with, even in the dormitories. The college was transformed into a home, and became, as it were, one great family, of which Mann was the kind and attentive father living in the midst of his children. The pupils were associated in the discipline of the house by a sort of mutual self-government. The oldest pupils took the younger ones under their special protection, just as in a family the big brothers look after the little ones, under the eye of the parents. At the convention of Ohio colleges in 1856 Mann offered the following resolution: "That the pupils in an institution of learning shall cooperate in its government and contribute toward maintaining order." This was very much what was being attempted at the same period at Rugby by the great English head-master, Thomas Arnold. At Antioch the students, on entering, pledged themselves on their honor to obey the rules of the college, and they kept their word. By appealing to their conscience, to their free will, Mann sought not only to fit them to be men, but to put an end to that state of warfare, that antagonism between teachers and pupils, which is so often the curse of education.

To avoid punishment as far as possible was the general aim of Mann's discipline; and he had explained himself fully upon this subject in his lecture of the year 1840. Punishment was an evil in his eyes: first, because under the pretext of preventing a greater evil it inflicts suffering; secondly, because it develops the sentiment of fear and thus debases mind and heart. Mann did not wish to make himself feared, but loved; and to obtain good work and order, he counted upon the affection which a kind and competent master inspires in his pupils, as well as upon the charms of learning and the interest aroused by well-taught lessons.

Without knowing Herbart he agreed with him when he says: "One hour a day spent by the professor in preparing an attractive lesson will dispense with many severities on his part." And elsewhere: "For a teacher to succeed he must have won the affection of his pupils. The child will learn nothing, not even mathematics, from a teacher he does not like." To express the depressing effects which a system of terror has on the mind, he says: "You cannot fail to have seen the trunk of an old tree bearing the scars of a wound it has received in its youth: all the wounded side has remained twisted and gnarled, whereas on the other side the tree, nourished by a superabundant sap, has attained a disproportionate size. This is the exact image of a man whose youth has been distorted by an excess of severity."

In cases where it is absolutely necessary to have recourse to punishment, — and Mann was fully aware that one must at times resign oneself to this course, — one should never forget that penal discipline should be merely repressive, that its aim is, above all, to amend the culprit and lead him back to the path of duty. Moreover, great care should be taken to proportion the penalty to the evil intention, the "will for evil" which the fault betrays; and, finally, one should resort to punishment only with regret and sorrow: "No punishment is beneficent except on condition of its being more painful to him who inflicts than to him who undergoes it."

For repressive discipline Mann therefore substituted a regime of trust and mildness. But such a regime supposes, on the part of him who applies it, strong moral authority joined to active vigilance. Every morning before prayers Mann delivered an address to the assembled pupils, — a sort of lay sermon, — which, however, did not dispense him from frequent private conversations with individual pupils and intimate, confidential talks.

His authority was reenforced by the sympathy he inspired, by his great powers of persuasion, and by the influence of his own conscientiousness. The noble ideal he set before his pupils was exemplified in his own laborious and stainless life. A pious American writer said of him: "He offered the radiant and rare example of a man in whom a religion of mere morality produces, or at least is united to, an ardor of feeling, an intensity of virtue, which are usually associated with faith and positive attachment to revealed religion."

"Where he was incomparable," writes one of his old pupils, "was in the art of arousing ardor and enthusiasm. It would be as impossible to be near the sun without feeling its warmth as to be a witness of Mann's passion for truth without sharing it. The vivacity of his impressions was merely one form of his faith in God and man, a faith so contagious that indifference, misanthropy, and scepticism vanished at his approach; and when he had communicated to us this ardor and this faith, he was so careful to respect our individuality that he put us on our guard against the ascendency which his own opinions might have gained over us. Thus we had in him as delicate a guide as he was a powerful inspirer. . . .

"We sometimes see free-thinkers who show themselves as intolerant toward any difference of opinion in their followers as are the bigots from whom they have parted company. But not so Mann; he was too conscious of this tendency in human nature to wish to indoctrinate others. He praised every effort in the direction of free thought; he distrusted no one who was seeking after truth in purity of heart and honesty of mind."

Does it not seem as if we were listening to an old pupil of Fontenay paying homage to Felix Pecaut and extolling at the same time the force of his moral ascendency and the delicate reserve and discretion of his liberal teaching? Does this imply that there is nothing to criticise in Mann's disciplinary methods? How can we approve of the role he assigned to his pupils when he urged them to report each other's misdoings? Just as in the social world a good citizen sets himself in opposition to the misdeeds he sees committed, so, according to Mann, in the smaller world of college a good student should prevent the evil he is aware of by reporting it. Was not this encouraging, to a certain extent, a habit of spying?

It is permissible, also, to hold that Mann obeyed the dictates of an extreme asceticism in the campaign which he conducted at Antioch, as elsewhere, against all infractions, even the most innocent ones, against the law of total abstinence. He had inherited a strain of Puritanism from his forefathers, and one can hardly refrain from smiling at the anathemas he launches with the utmost solemnity against tobacco and smokers; as, for example, when he says to the Antioch students: "It is not mere smoke, young men, which you see floating off in cloudy spirals, it is a part of your souls; when your nerves become impregnated with tobacco, they can no longer execute your will."

In his somewhat prejudiced campaign against tobacco, he found no less than ten reasons for proscribing its use; to wit, that tobacco is injurious to the health; that it poisons the air and annoys non-smokers; that it is a dirty and also a costly habit; that for the amount a smoker spends for his tobacco he could buy a farm, build a house, or, at the very least, collect a library, etc. The drinking habit has never had in the United States a more implacable adversary than Mann. During the convention of the Ohio Teachers' Association, he caused the following resolution to be adopted on December 27, 1836:

"School examiners shall never grant a certificate of fitness as an instructor to any one indulging in the habitual use of spirituous liquors; and where the qualifications are equal between candidates, the preference shall be systematically given to the candidate who is a total abstainer."

But on how many points Mann gave evidence of the broadest spirit, notably in regard to the education of woman. "The coeducation of the sexes," he said, "is our great experiment at Antioch." He had already attempted it — and with success — in two of his primary normal schools in Massachusetts. He now sought to introduce in a college or institution of secondary education a reform which he regarded as an excellent one, and which his countrymen have since widely adopted. In fact, at the present day coeducation is the rule rather than the exception in schools of every order in the United States. And in the higher, or university, education also, Mann advocated the mingling of both sexes, as he set forth in a statement addressed to the University of Michigan, the first university to adopt the principle of coeducation. Already in Ohio, at Oberlin College, women were admitted as students, but not without restrictions: they were not allowed to participate in the complete scholastic course, but merely permitted to follow a two years' term of study. At Antioch, Mann went farther, — he opened wide the college gates to girls. He held an exalted view of woman and resented the old-time prejudices which denied her the higher education on the pretext that she had no need for it, or was incapable of profiting by it, and that she was devoid of natural aptitude for the sciences. How frequently he spoke in praise of the feminine qualities in terms which prove the delicacy of his own sentiments, while honoring the noble-hearted women whom he had known, and who served him as models when he drew this portrait:

"Woman walks henceforth by the side of man, associated with him in his work of regeneration; she is always gentle, gracious, and filled with lofty ideas of duty. Unequalled in all deeds of kindness and charity, she binds up man's wounds with a hand unhardened by wielding deadly weapons, while her heart glows with the divine desire to make peace and purity reign upon earth."

When Mann wrote these beautiful words, he was doubtless inspired by the example of her who was the companion of his later years, and who, after his death, showed a pious and touching devotion to his memory.

Thus Mann invited women to seat themselves on the same collegiate benches and to live beneath the same roof with young men at Antioch, and he found no cause to regret the step. At the convention of Ohio colleges in 1855, he recorded the results of his experiment in the following words: "Each sex has exercised a salutary influence over the other; they have stimulated each other intellectually and sustained each other morally."

These are the reasons still given by the partisans of coeducation, not only in America, but in England, where a movement in favor of mixed colleges has prevailed for several years. In presence of girls, the youths, who have become their comrades in study, are roused to emulation; they wish by their success to maintain the honor of their sex, in which laudable design they are not always successful; for, according to American opinion, it is the girls who are most frequently at the head of the classes. But at least the young men are spurred on to greater efforts, while their manners are softened and their language and bearing are freed from coarseness. The girls, on the other hand, lay aside their natural timidity and all that is essentially effeminate in their character; they gain in strength as much as do their comrades of the sterner sex in gentleness and courtesy.

Mann was aware, however, that coeducation, while presenting many advantages, entails also certain dangers. To prevent these, he took all manner of precautions, knowing that the success of such a regime depends greatly upon the vigilance of the presiding head. He gave, accordingly, to the young men and women of Antioch opportunities for meeting frequently in evening gatherings and friendly reunions in presence of their teachers, seeking in this way to encourage general social intercourse among them and counteract the tendency to seek tete-a-tetes and private interviews. That the attainment of final diplomas was not always the soul object of the students, both youths and maidens, of Antioch, and that more than one matrimonial engagement enlivened the monotony of these studies in common, it would be vain to deny. But Mann would have retorted, like the Americans of our own day, What harm in that? From this comradeship in studies may result the best assorted unions between young people, who have learned to know each other, to study each other's characters, and to draw from their mutual sympathy as schoolmates the elements of future conjugal affection.

Let us add that Mann, while offering to young men and young girls the privileges of equal education, did not desire that it should be identical. He did not admit the idea that education in common should case the two sexes in the same mould; he considered that woman should be brought up as woman, that she should not "wear a mustache nor sing bass."

The experiments tried by Mann at Antioch in coeducation, as in all else, appear to have been attended with complete success. Antioch was regarded as the first of Western colleges, with which no other would bear comparison. Mann, had he lived long enough, would have joyfully continued his experiments in liberal education, and thus have contributed to the general progress of humanity.

With the advance of age his devotion to men only waxed greater in a heart which always remained young. In 1856 he wrote to George Combe:

"I am sixty years old; I am too deeply interested in the great affair of human progress to wish to die. Those great vital questions of pauperism, peace, and slavery, of temperance and education, I cannot leave behind without a painful rending of the very fibres of my heart. You will doubtless tell me that these things will go on of themselves. But I should like to see them go on with my own eyes, while I am alive. I am impatient to watch their advance. I feel for these noble causes what a father feels for the children he loves, when he dreads leaving them before they are secure from all moral dangers."

It was not to be granted to Mann to cooperate longer in the progress of the great movements to which he had devoted his life. His end was approaching; and to the very last day, he labored and struggled with the difficulties of a financial situation which was going from bad to worse.

In 1858 failure was imminent; the ruin of the college appeared certain. Mann succeeded, however, in averting it by mortgaging the house he owned in West Newton, and by appealing for aid to various generous friends. A new corporation was formed, and the college was saved. But it was too late. Mann's days were numbered; he died on the 2d of August, 1859.[1]

His physical strength, which he had greatly overtaxed, had long been failing. On the 28th

---

[1] Mann's successor as president of Antioch was Dr. Thomas Hill. The college was suspended during the Civil War, from 1861–1865, but was opened immediately on its conclusion, and has remained to this day a flourishing institution under the direction of Unitarians.

of April, 1859, being invited to the first convention of the normal schools of America, he replied:

"Public schools were my first love; they will be my last. But I must seek to recover my health; I am worn out, *abolished*, by hard labor. I am a white slave who cannot look, alas! for any abolition of his slavery." He realized that his days were numbered. In his last address, delivered after the examinations of 1859 — what the Americans call the Baccalaureate sermon — and which was his swan-song, he said:

"Girls and young men, after so many years passed together on our journey of life, the moment of separation has come. In a day, in an hour, we shall part. Would that I might continue to walk beside you, to sustain you with look and voice in the struggle against ignorance and selfishness on which you are about to enter! Up, then, and onward, my young friends! When, after my experience of life, I am asked what I would do if I were allowed to issue it again in a revised edition, I answer that I should wish to do more and better in works of humanity, temperance, peace, education, — especially the education of women. I should like to live again, to enroll myself anew in a fifty years' campaign, and fight once more for the glory of God and the happiness of humanity!"

Mann's death was a touching one: the death of a Socrates, with the added presence of a beloved wife and cherished sons. The physicians warned him that he had but three hours more to live, as the jailer of Athens announced that the hour for drinking the hemlock had come. The dying man raised himself upon his bed of pain and for two hours conversed feverishly with the faithful friends, the weeping pupils, who surrounded him. His last words testified to the serenity of a strong soul who controls the final agonies in his thoughts for those he is about to leave, and who affirms for the last time the faith and sentiments which have always inspired him. Of one of his favorite pupils who was absent he said: "Dear Carey, always good, always upright, always firm, tell him how I love him! Those good young men who always do their duty, how I love them! Tell them how I love them!" Then addressing another pupil whom he held in especial esteem: "Preach the laws of God; preach them till their light penetrates the darkness of the world." At last the agony began, during which Mann pronounced only broken words: "Man — God — Duty." Then death arrived, not calm and peaceful but tormented, agitated, as the life had been. "It was hard for that powerful brain to die!" At least until his last hour Mann had preserved his lucidity of mind and proclaimed his faith, remaining to the end an apostle, a prophet, — the prophet of the happiness of men through virtue.

V

HORACE MANN'S INFLUENCE AND THE SPREAD OF HIS WORK

IF it were granted to Horace Mann to live again and revisit this world, he would doubtless find some subjects for disappointment and bitterness. Were he to make once more, fifty years later, his European trip, he would discover with grief the distressing increase, in some countries at least, of the curse of alcoholism. He would read with pain, in the newspapers of his own country, that "the horrors of intemperance are the greatest evil of American life." And, above all, he, the friend of peace among men, the "pacificator," as we say to-day, with what sorrowful eyes would he behold the military spirit and its formidable armaments increasing even in the United States.

On the other hand, what joy the abolition of slavery would cause him. He died three years before the outbreak of the civil war of 1861–1865. He would have been saddened by the bloody violence of that fratricidal strife, but would have rejoiced over its results, since it put an end to the institution of slavery, which he held in such abhorrence. But, above all, if he could contemplate to-day the magnificent growth of popular education in all countries, particularly his own, the apostle of education would certainly feel happiness and pride in the spread and progress of his ideas, while admitting, doubtless, that the efforts of his successors have been powerless up to this time in abolishing the evil in the world, and that humanity, in spite of having grown more learned and enlightened, is still a long way from attaining that ideal of happiness and virtue of which he had dreamed.

For half a century the United States have faithfully conformed in the matter of public education to the programme which Mann had traced for them. He had wished to see the schoolhouses habitable, comfortable, even architecturally fine, and America has clothed herself with scholastic palaces, which none of her children dream of criticising. He desired free schools, with the schooling obligatory; and one no longer sees in America those paying public schools, which he called the "blot on our civilization." The poor school has disappeared, and, moreover, vigorous efforts have been made that obligatory education should not be a mere name, certain States going so far as to refuse the rights of suffrage to the illiterate. He desired the common school to be universal, frequented by the children of the rich as well as of the destitute, in order that aristocratic prejudices should fade away, which separate in institutions of learning the children of one country, and which too long forbade the sons of well-to-do citizens from sitting on the same school benches with the sons of farmers and workingmen. For any citizen not to send his children to the public schools on the pretext that he is rich and that these schools are open gratuitously to all, appeared to Mann to be treason against democracy. In this direction, also, progress is apparent, though still incomplete. He was averse to introducing any positive religious instruction into the school, regarding the teaching of dogmas as despotism on the master's part and servitude on that of the scholars. He almost grasped the necessity of an absolutely and purely lay school; for while he admitted the reading of the Bible, he forbade accompanying it with any commentary. At the present day, although America, amid its diversity of sects, has remained more faithful to its ancient religious faith than certain European countries, there are, nevertheless, numbers of American educators who would go farther than Mann, and who are disposed to exclude from the schools even the reading of the Bible. "If there are children who do not wish to read the Bible," they say, "the Bible should not be inscribed on the school programme."

Mann was the first secretary of a regularly established board of education in the United States, and to-day there does not exist within the great American Union a single State which does not possess, under one form or another, a central authority established for the supervision and direction of the public schools. Sometimes it is a board of education similar to the Boston one; sometimes it consists merely of a single head, a superintendent; in the Western States a county superintendent, in the East a city superintendent and, moreover, with widely different powers. One such superintendent corresponds to our provincial minister of public instruction, another is merely the director of a bureau of information and statistics. But everywhere, taught by Mann's example, the Americans have established an official authority who presides over the destiny of schools, and it would appear that at this very moment a movement is started to extend its action and reenforce its powers.

Progress in school organization, progress in administration — all this, however, has not been accomplished in a day. The United States have not, like France, a centralized government, where an order from above, a national law, can, from one day to the next, transform the entire system of education and impose uniform and universal rules over its whole territory. Each State in the Union has its individual spirit and character, and by the very reason of their diversity of manners and social condition, they have not all advanced at an equal pace along the path of progress. Just as on a summer night the stars shine forth in the sky one after another, according to their magnitude and position in space, so the States of the American Union have set in motion their scholastic enterprises successively and gradually, according to their resources and their degree of advancement in the march of civilization. It is the Eastern States that have led the way, but the Western States have followed with such rapid strides that they no longer have anything for which to envy their precursors.[1]

To the appeal of Mann, of Barnard, and all their followers, the United States have made a superb response. At the dawn of the twentieth century, they offer to the admiration of the world an en-

[1] Ohio had appointed a superintendent in 1837, three months before the establishment of the Boston Board.

semble of scholastic institutions which no other country can surpass.[1] They assemble in their public schools of the first grade more than 15,000,000 children, as many as the total population of Spain. The teachers in these institutions, men and women, number 426,000, and the annual expenditure is $212,000,000, *i.e.* over a billion francs, as much as France expends in maintaining her army and navy.

Mann, whatever may have been the ardor of his hopes, would have stood amazed before this marvellous effort. To speak of Massachusetts alone, the State to which he communicated the most vigorous impulse, what a change and what progress in fifty years! In 1848 the budget of that State for common school education did not exceed $700,000; it now reaches more than $11,000,000. In 1848 Massachusetts possessed but three normal schools, those with which Mann had endowed the State; they number ten to-day. The school population has risen from 185,000 children in 1848 to 424,000 in 1896. And, finally, the number of men and women teachers has increased from 7924 to 12,275 (of whom 11,197 are women to 1078 men).

[1] Among the causes to which the United States owe the admirable progress in primary education, we must note the abolition of slavery, which opened the way for public schools in sixteen new States.

Two ideas equally dear to Mann's heart, coeducation and instruction by women, have become more and more acclimated in the United States. In Massachusetts, as we have shown in the figures quoted above, the proportion is eleven women teachers to one man, and it is nearly the same all over America.[1] As to coeducation, it does not cease to make progress, and is in general favor, not only in the public schools, but even in colleges and universities. It has become — and how Mann would rejoice thereat ! — a characteristic feature of the American school system. Mann was concerned not only with the elementary public schools, he was equally interested in schools of the second degree, such as are called in America high schools. The first high school was founded in Boston in 1821; Mann occupied himself with starting others, and to-day, on the showing of Mr. Harris, the eminent director of the Washington Board of Education, the increase in the number of high schools is perhaps the most important event in the history of education in the United States during the last years of the nineteenth century. This progress was for a long time slow and imperceptible. In 1860 the whole United States

[1] In certain cities the proportion in favor of women is even higher. In Philadelphia, in 1899, 3174 women were teaching to 190 men.

counted but 40 schools of this type, to more than 800 in 1880. But in the last twenty years of the nineteenth century, American intermediate education received an immense impetus; in fact, the number of high schools in 1900 was about 6000, with more than 500,000 pupils, boys and girls — 244 of these schools being in Massachusetts alone.[1]

If Mann's influence, after the lapse of fifty years, still pervades the scholastic institutions of the United States, it was especially during his lifetime that it was powerful and effective. Nor was it in the State of Massachusetts alone that he exercised this influence. Before he had carried his scholastic gospel in person to the Mississippi Valley, his writings, and especially his school reports, had circulated far and wide. "Mann's reports," wrote George B. Emerson, in 1844, "have waked an echo in the woods of Maine, on the banks of the St. Lawrence, on the shores of the Great Lakes. They have been read and listened to in New York, in the West and Southwest. The importance they have acquired is shown by the fact

---

[1] It is to be noticed, moreover, that the number of girls in the high schools considerably surpasses that of boys, — 200,000 boys only to 300,000 girls, — which is to be regretted, since, according to the testimony of its warmest defenders, coeducation has full efficacy only in schools where the proportion between the sexes is about equal.

that a man from Massachusetts has been selected to organize the schools of New Orleans. At this very moment his reports are regenerating the Rhode Island schools, while in the remotest corners of Ohio forty people have been known to meet to read together the only copy of the Boston secretary's reports which they had been able to obtain."

The worth of a great man is recognized in this, —that he founds a school and raises up imitators and disciples. Mann inspired one such disciple, who became almost his equal, and shares with him the honor of having led the pedagogic movement in the United States in the nineteenth century. This was Henry Barnard, of whom Mann said in 1850, "If one wishes to find a more capable man than he, one must wait for the next generation." Barnard was in turn school superintendent of Connecticut from 1832 to 1842, State superintendent for Rhode Island from 1843 to 1849, president of St. John's College from 1858 to 1867, and, finally, commissioner of the Board of Education in Washington from 1867 to 1870. His career offers many analogies with that of Mann: if the latter was prominent in the reform of asylums for the insane, Barnard labored equally for prison reform and for the reorganization of institutions for the blind and deaf and dumb. The great American educators have always extended their solicitude to the infirm, the abnormal, — to those disinherited by nature.

Barnard published for forty years the *American Journal of Education,* a real encyclopædia of pedagogy from the historical, as well as the doctrinal, point of view. He had but one claim to superiority over Mann, — that of a longer life, since born in 1811, he died, full of years, in 1901.

Mann's countrymen have not forgotten what they owe him. They have raised statues to him, and in 1897 they celebrated the anniversary of his birth; but what is better still is that they remain faithful to his inspiration, and he may be said to be still present in their midst. It may be said also that his spirit has penetrated into Europe and particularly into France. It will not be detracting from the honor due to the organizers of elementary instruction in France under the Third Republic to say that they were in great measure inspired by the thought and example of the great American educator. To mention but one, our Pecaut, above all, appears to us as a French Horace Mann, more impressive, of a deeper and more intense inner life, more reserved and discreet; a Horace Mann without the gift of oratory, but with greater moderation and delicacy of mental quality, worthy in any case to figure, like him, in the front rank in the golden book of great modern educators.

BIBLIOGRAPHY

THERE can be no question here of giving a complete bibliography of Mann's works, nor especially of the five or six hundred books and pamphlets published about him. Let us cite merely the principal editions of his writings and the most important of the studies which have appeared regarding his work.

HORACE MANN, *Reports as Secretary of the Board of Education of Massachusetts*, 12 vols. Boston, 1838–1849.

The same, abridged and edited by GEORGE COMBE MANN, 4 vols. Boston, 1891.

HORACE MANN, *Lectures on Education*, 1 vol. Boston, 1845.

MARY MANN, *Life of Horace Mann, by his Wife*, 1st edition. Boston, 1865.

MARY MANN, *Life and Works of Horace Mann*, 5 vols. Cambridge, 1867.

In the Reports of the Commissioner of Education, published in Washington, will be found a series of studies upon Horace Mann. We will point out two particularly important ones.

Horace Mann, by Mr. W. T. HARRIS; notice followed by a bibliography made out by one of Mann's sons, Mr. B. Pickman Mann, and which, although incomplete, comprises no less than 600 different publications (Reports, etc., 1895–1896, pp. 886–927).

Horace Mann and the Great Revival of the American Common School, by A. D. MAYO. (Reports, etc., 1896–1897, pp. 715–767).

BARNARD, *Horace Mann*. Hartford, 1858.

HINSDALE, *Horace Mann and Public Education in the United States*, in the collection *The Great Educators*. New York, 1898.

French works: —

LABOULAYE, *Lecture on the Importance of Education in a Republic*. Paris, 1873.

GAUFRES, *Horace Mann, his Work, his Writings*, 1 vol. Paris, Hachette, 2d edition, 1897.

FELIX PECAUT, article in the *Revue pedagogique*, 1888, vol. 1.

Made in United States
North Haven, CT
09 March 2024